D0127506

AMERICAN SANDWICH

GREAT EATS FROM AMERICAN

SANDWICH

Becky Mercuri

GIBBS SMITH

Gibbs Smith, Publisher
Salt Lake City

First Edition
08 07 06 05 04 5 4 3 2 1

Text © 2004 Becky Mercuri

All rights reserved. No part of this book may be reproduced by any means whatsoever without written permission from the publisher, except brief portions quoted for purpose of review.

Published by
Gibbs Smith, Publisher
P.O. Box 667
Layton, Utah 84041

1.800.748.5439 orders
www.gibbs-smith.com

Designed and produced by Kurt Wahlner
Printed and bound in Korea

Library of Congress Cataloging-in-Publication Data

Mercuri, Becky.
  The great American sandwich book / Becky Mercuri.—1st ed.
      p. cm.
  Includes index.
  ISBN 1-58685-470-4
  1. Sandwiches. 2. Cookery, American. I. Title.
TX818.M48 2004
641.8'4—dc22
2004005053

Contents

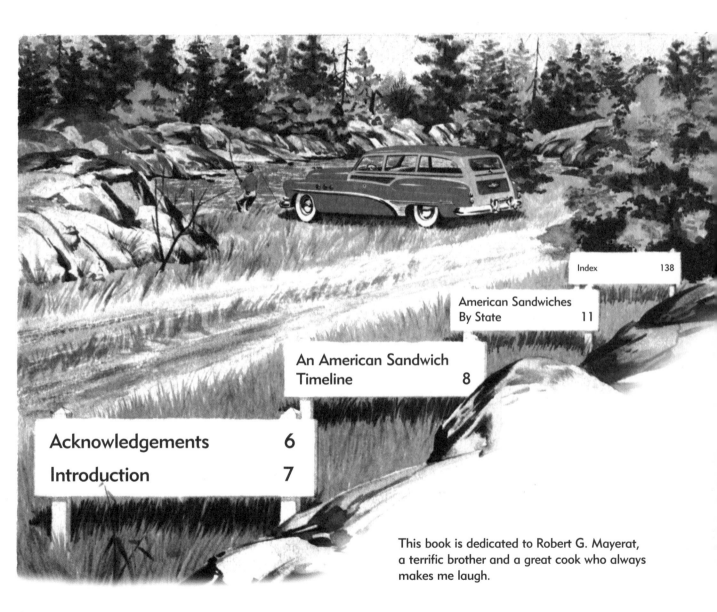

This book is dedicated to Robert G. Mayerat,
a terrific brother and a great cook who always
makes me laugh.

Acknowledgments

WRITING ABOUT American cooking and foodways has taken me down many a twisted path, always leading to exciting historical information, delicious recipes, and interesting people. Even a telephone call may herald a new adventure, as happened one fine day when none other than Gibbs Smith and Suzanne Taylor of Gibbs Smith, Publisher, telephoned. Having just viewed **Sandwiches That You Will Like**, produced by Rick Sebak of WQED in Pittsburgh, Gibbs and Suzanne wanted to know more about America's sandwich culture and the companion cookbook and sandwich history that I had written. The result of that conversation was a whirlwind tour of some of America's best restaurants, the discovery of the signature sandwiches of these establishments, and this book, filled with fabulous recipes that bring a true taste of America into home kitchens. I'm grateful for Gibbs' and Suzanne's vision, enthusiasm, and support.

I am indebted, as always, to Barry Popik, one of the most extraordinary etymological and food researchers of our time, for his boundless energy, dedication, and perseverance in tracking down historical information related to so many of the sandwiches featured herein. Until recently, food history was not considered a serious area of study, comparatively little information was recorded by past generations, and research is often difficult, at best. Barry's unflagging dedication has lead to the discovery of new resources and archives and his ultimate disproving of "urban legends" that did not accurately portray American foodways and cuisine.

I am deeply grateful to the many restaurant owners and chefs who so generously shared the recipes for their signature sandwiches—their names appear throughout this book. As patrons and consumers, we can be proud of these people who have dedicated a healthy dose of creativity, a sense of tradition, and a respect for the finest of ingredients, all of which has culminated in a uniquely American sandwich culture.

Special thanks and appreciation are extended to those who suggested restaurants and sandwiches for inclusion in this book: Pasquale "Pat" Bruno, Rick Sebak, John T. Edge, Margaret Mayerat, Chef Michael Sigler, Holly Moore, John Thorne, Chuck Taggart, Glenn Lindgren, Raúl Musibay, Jorge Castilla, Bill Green, Margaret Jo Borland Beckwith, Marci Penner, Judy and Matthew Amster, Tim Dotson, and Andi Flanagan.

Special thanks go to my agent, Meredith Bernstein, and to Patty Walker at WQED Multimedia in Pittsburgh. I sincerely appreciate the great support of editors Madge Baird and Linda Nimori at Gibbs Smith, Publisher. Finally, testing recipes requires curious palates, a sense of adventure, and hearty appetites. I thank Richard Boas and Tony Green for all of that and more.

Introduction

AMERICA is a nation of sandwich eaters. We commonly live life in the fast lane, and we necessarily dote on food that is portable. The sandwich has thus become a mainstay of our existence. Sandwiches are to Americans what pasta is to Italians or what tortillas are to Mexicans. Sandwich shops are everywhere. Take-out and delivery are not just window dressing for many such businesses; they are integral to attracting and keeping a loyal clientele who commonly lunch at their desks or even behind the wheels of their cars. Even when eating in restaurants, Americans love sandwiches, and not just for lunch. Sandwiches are now common offerings for breakfast, and up-scale sandwich creations are even appearing on dinner menus. In two-income households, harried parents often turn to sandwiches as a quick and convenient family meal.

Although the sandwich was invented by a notorious English gambler, John Montagu, the Fourth Earl of Sandwich, nowhere else on earth has it become so ingrained in a national cuisine. Indeed, American travelers are often shocked to find that the sandwich is seldom as commonly available abroad as it is at home.

American sandwiches have evolved from dainty offerings at afternoon tea, a custom we inherited from the English, to providing a filling and nutritious meal. Along the way, immigrants to America had a profound influence on our sandwich culture by introducing hearty sandwiches that sustained factory workers, policemen, and coal miners. In some cases, immigrants modified a recipe from their homeland in a way that appealed to Americans while creating a way to earn a living in their new home. Innovative cooks and chefs were responsible for introducing other unique sandwiches. In many cases, these sandwiches have become so popular that they now enjoy recognized regional or national stature. Americans everywhere are wont to talk about their favorite sandwiches with great fondness, and many affectionately refer to them as sangwiches, sandriches, sangwidges, sammidges, or sammies.

It's generally agreed that there are four basic components to a sandwich: the bread, the spread, the filling, and the garnish. While most people believe that the filling is the most important of the four, it's hard to imagine a really great sandwich without the rest, especially good bread.

You won't find haute cuisine in this book. But you will find truly great American sandwiches. And you'll find both plain and fancy restaurants, all with character, good food, and friendly people. You'll also find recipes for some of America's greatest sandwiches, many having been enjoyed for decades. Several of these sandwiches have interesting stories behind their creation, and some have more than one claim as to who was responsible for their invention. The history of others has been lost in time. Still others are new creations reflecting changing tastes and new ingredients. They are all a true taste of America. Enjoy!

Becky Mercuri
January 2004

IT IS MOST LIKELY that sandwiches date back to the time when civilization and the establishment of permanent settlements occurred in the Middle East, around 9000 BC. Grain was planted and harvested, providing the major ingredient for unleavened bread that was first baked over an open fire. Flatbreads, as they later came to be called, would have provided a natural means for conveying food from hand to mouth, holding whatever was at hand: a piece of roasted meat or perhaps some dried fish. And flatbread, as a container of sorts, allowed for ease in transporting food destined to be eaten as workers or travelers journeyed from place to place. It's entirely possible that the biblical reference to "loaves and fishes" pointed to sandwiches that stretched the food at hand and thus fed the multitudes. Certainly, as yeast making was discovered and bread evolved into myriad forms, it became the staff of life for millions of people throughout the centuries.

According to J. J. Schnebel, an Internet researcher, the French claim that it had long been common for both travelers and field workers to carry with them meat or fish between two slices of black bread well before the English coined the term "sandwich." Perhaps the sandwich, per se, was commonly eaten by the European lower classes, whose eating habits, let alone their "recipes," were rarely, if ever, recorded in those days. And maybe it took the stamp of approval, given by the Earl of Sandwich, to make his namesake socially acceptable to the aristocracy, at least in England.

Which brings us to the "creation" of the sandwich itself. John Montagu (1718–1792), the Fourth Earl of Sandwich, is commonly credited with its invention. A notorious gambler and rogue also known as "Jemmy Twitcher," the Earl was frequently reluctant to interrupt his marathon card games and perhaps his good-luck streak as well. It is said that Montagu was the first person to order sliced meat placed between two pieces of bread, an event that reportedly occurred in 1762 at London's Beef Steak Club, situated above Covent Garden Theatre. The ability to eat his sandwich one-handed left the Earl a free hand for playing cards.

America's close ties with England, even after the American Revolution, were reflected in much of our early cuisine. English colonists brought their foodways with them and adapted their cooking in order to accommodate both new-world foodstuffs and those they were able to obtain from the old world. The few cookbooks in existence during those early years in America were mostly English imports, and even American authors tended to imitate, if not outright plagiarize, material from cookbooks written by their English counterparts.

With the publication of **Miss Leslie's Directions for Cookery** in 1837, Eliza Leslie was apparently the first person to formally introduce the sandwich to America. Born in Philadelphia in 1787, Miss Leslie spent her youth in England, where she may have encountered the sandwich. Her cookbook featured the following recipe for ham sandwiches:

Ham Sandwiches

Cut some thin slices of bread very neatly, having slightly buttered them; and, if you choose, spread on a very little mustard. Have ready some very thin slices of cold boiled ham, and lay on between two slices of bread. You may either roll them up, or lay them flat on the plates. They are used at supper, or at luncheon.

By the 1860s, sandwiches were commonly served as simple supper fare, and they were often packed in travelers' knapsacks. Supper, of course, was a relatively light meal since the main meal of the day, known in those days as dinner, was held at midday.

An American Sandwich Timeline

As light fare for luncheons, suppers, or picnics, sandwiches continued to be comprised mainly of thinly sliced ham placed between equally thin slices of bread until 1884. That was the year that Mrs. D. A. Lincoln, the first principal of the Boston Cooking School, wrote the very first version of the **Boston Cooking School Cook Book.** It became the standard by which all other cookbooks of the period were judged, and it presented more variety in sandwich fillings, including cooked ham, corned beef, or tongue; lobster or chicken salad sandwiches; and raw beef sandwiches, recommended for invalids "who could not otherwise take raw meat."

In 1896, Lincoln's cookbook was followed by **The Original Boston Cooking-School Cook Book** by Fannie Merritt Farmer, and it actually included an entire chapter devoted to sandwiches. Both white and brown breads were recommended, and Farmer gave instructions for such fillings as sardines, anchovies, fried oysters, jelly, nut and cheese, and fruit. However, these were still not the hearty sandwiches that we know today, but dainty, fussy concoctions based on spreads and thinly carved meats. With crusts removed from bread that was often cut in decorative shapes, this was food destined for the tea tables of polite Victorian society.

During the first two decades of the twentieth century, sandwiches continued to evolve, and they were made with an ever-increasing array of fillings. Of importance is the fact that several of our most famous sandwiches were actually created by immigrants during this period, even though they would not take their place in the mainstream of American foodways for several years.

In the 1920s, technology ushered in a veritable sandwich revolution. On May 24, 1921, Wonder Bread, "the new wrapped loaf," festooned with those famous red, yellow, and blue balloons, was introduced to the American market with great fanfare. It was named "Wonder" because of its one-and-a-half-pound size. With ready-made bread generally available, Americans increased their sandwich consumption as a major part of meals, and people began referring to white bread as "sandwich bread" or as a "sandwich loaf."

Two other technological innovations ensured the success of the sandwich in America's culinary repertoire. The first pop-up toaster, called the "Toastmaster," was introduced in 1926 for use in the American home. Presliced bread, first marketed by Wonder Bread in 1930, accounted for nearly 80 percent of the bread sold in the United States by 1933, and Americans were so enthusiastic about it that the expression "the best thing since sliced bread" was coined. Clearly, both the toaster and sliced bread paved the way for the wave of sandwiches that would follow and that would be embraced by an adoring American public.

During the 1920s, luncheonettes serving sandwiches began popping up everywhere. There was even a popular song, "A Cup of Coffee, a Sandwich and You," released by Billy Rose and Al Dubin in 1925, which paid a kind of romantic tribute to the sandwich. By the late 1920s and the early 1930s, sandwiches had become more robust, often made from heavier breads and rolls with hearty fillings. Sold from pushcarts to hardworking immigrant laborers and fueled by

the hard times of the depression era, sandwiches were an inexpensive but complete meal. They could be ordered at most lunch counters across the United States, and people packed them in their lunch boxes as a convenient portable food.

The popularity of the sandwich in America was positively impacted by other technological changes as well. Affordable automobiles meant that Americans were on the move, and travelers needed to eat. This spawned the American drive-in restaurants that sprang up throughout the country. In **The American Drive-In Restaurant,** author Michael Karl Witzel recounts the story of that first successful drive-in eatery, the Pig Stand, opened in 1921 just off the busy Dallas–Fort Worth Highway. Its creators, Jessie G. Kirby and Reuben Jackson, had assessed the mentality of America's car owners, deciding they were too lazy to get out and eat. And, indeed, travelers as well as locals out for a drive and a meal were delighted with the fast carhop service, the ability to eat in the privacy of their own vehicle (a special bonus for parents with small children), and the tasty sandwiches that made a great alternative to the generally below-average food that travelers had previously endured.

While the Pig Stand specialized in pork sandwiches, it wasn't long before other drive-ins with various sandwich and drink specialties sprang up throughout the United States. A&W Root Beer opened its doors in 1919 in Lodi, California, and many more such establishments, under various names, followed. The mainstay of the new road food eventually became the hamburger, accompanied by french fries, soft drinks, and milk shakes. But it was enough to firmly establish sandwiches as ultimately acceptable in the American psyche.

Although America's entry into World War II in 1941 necessarily meant rationing, the popularity of the sandwich continued. Sandwiches once again assumed their depression-era role of providing nourishing, inexpensive, and filling meals eaten in American homes and carried off to factories by workers employed in America's essential war industry.

When the war was over and American soldiers returned home, they brought with them a taste for foods with an international flavor. Previously scorned as "foreign food" by many Americans, sandwiches born in other cultures and countries and brought to America by immigrants were suddenly in demand. The Philadelphia Cheese Steak sandwich and Chicago's Italian Beef sandwich joined the lexicon of popular regional delights. Americans' increasingly sophisticated palates also provided a warm welcome for new sandwiches introduced by later immigrants, like the Cubans who fled the Castro government in the late 1950s, bringing their Cuban sandwiches with them, or like the Vietnamese who introduced the Bãhn Mi when they arrived in the 1970s. And as Americans traveled throughout the country, they discovered other regional favorites such as the Maine Lobster Roll, the New Orleans Muffaletta, the California French Dip, and the Texas Chicken Fried Steak sandwich. Today, these and other major American cities and states are identified with a special sandwich indigenous to the area.

The Wheat Foods Council declared 2002 as the "Year of the Sandwich," honoring its creation 240 years previously by John Montagu, the Fourth Earl of Sandwich. This clever public-relations strategy clearly recognized the importance of America's sandwich culture. As the council pointed out, Americans eat more than 45 billion sandwiches per year, with the average American consuming 193 sandwiches annually. With new sandwiches continually being introduced and embraced by an adoring public, America is clearly in the throes of a "sandwich explosion."

AMERICAN

By State

SANDWICH

Approximately half the peanuts produced in the United States are grown within a hundred-mile radius of Dothan, Alabama, which bills itself as the "Peanut Capital of the World." Located in the southeastern part of the state known as the Wiregrass area, the region's 1,200 peanut farmers have been honored every November since 1938 at the National Peanut Festival. Visitors to Dothan are greeted by a giant gold peanut sculpture at the Visitor Information Center, and scattered throughout the city, one encounters five-foot-high fiberglass peanut sculptures, each whimsically decorated to represent a special theme or character. A series of spectacular murals in historic downtown Dothan commemorate area events, people, and places, including one dedicated to the National Peanut Festival and Dr. George Washington Carver, who developed over three hundred uses for the peanut.

Although the creation of peanut butter dates to 1890, it wasn't produced commercially until 1922 when a revolutionary new churning process was introduced, delivering a smoother, stabilized product with a longer shelf life. The increasing popularity of peanut butter dovetailed with the broad distribution of presliced bread in the early 1930s, but it wasn't until World War II that peanut butter was combined with jelly in sandwiches. It's believed that American soldiers first combined the two ingredients, commonly found in their ration kits, because the jelly made it easier to eat the sticky peanut butter. By the end of the war, peanut butter was a kitchen staple, and with the end of sugar rationing, Welch's Grape Jelly became its choice companion.

In Dothan, Alabama, peanut butter fans are likely to head for the Basketcase Café, where owners Donna and Rick Balzaretti produce a veritable parade of creative signature dishes. Boosters of local peanut production, their substantial lunch sandwich menu features a big seller: the P B & J Bama Cristo, a delicious version of two classic American favorites, the peanut butter and jelly sandwich and the Monte Cristo.

P B & J BAMA CRISTO

Reprinted with permission from Donna Balzaretti, chef and owner of the Basketcase Café, Dothan, Alabama

Canola oil or cooking spray

1 egg

2 tablespoons milk

3 1/2 teaspoons peanut butter

2 1/2 teaspoons apple jelly

2 slices Texas toast (quality white bread sliced 1 inch thick and toasted)

2 slices bacon, fried crisp and drained

WHERE TO GO:

Basketcase Café
228 South Oates Street
Dothan, AL 36301
(334) 671-1117

National Peanut Festival
5622 Highway 231 South
Dothan, AL 36301
(334) 793-4323
www.nationalpeanutfestival.com

IF DEEP-FRYING THE SANDWICH, heat cooking oil to a depth of 2 inches in a deep, heavy frying pan until it reaches 350 degrees.

In a shallow bowl wide enough for dipping the sandwich, prepare batter by beating together the egg and milk. In a small bowl, mix the peanut butter and apple jelly. Spread the peanut butter mixture on one slice of the toast, top with bacon, and cover with the remaining slice of toast. Press the sandwich together lightly. Dip the sandwich in the batter until coated on both sides.

Deep-fry the sandwich in the hot fat, or fry on a griddle that has been preheated and greased with cooking spray, about 30 seconds on each side, or until golden brown. Drain the sandwich on paper towels, slice in half, and serve immediately.

Yield: 1 sandwich

MAIN STREET, DOTHAN, ALABAMA

327 POUND HALIBUT LENGTH 8'2" WIDTH 4'6' CAUGHT BY CAPT. OSCAR OBERG AND CREW IN HYPERION APRIL 29-29.

Alaska's seafood industry is the state's largest private employer, and the majority of America's halibut harvest comes from Alaskan waters. History records the first shipment of fresh halibut from Juneau in 1897, and by 2000, Alaskan halibut fisheries reported production levels of 85 million pounds. While much of the halibut catch is shipped to the "Lower 48," a goodly portion is reserved for the local market. Its flaky texture and mild, buttery flavor may account for the Middle English term halybutte, referring to the fact that the flatfish was to be eaten on holy days.

Alaskans are fond of introducing visitors (known as cheechakos, or newcomers) to the delights of Alaskan seafood specialties like salmon and halibut. The latter is found in everything from fish tacos to fish fries, and halibut sandwiches, called "buttwiches" in the local vernacular, are a favorite throughout the state. Humpy's Great Alaskan Alehouse in Anchorage is a popular watering hole that's also known for its terrific halibut burgers. Named for one of the original owners of Humpy's, the sandwich is served up with a good dollop of Humpy's homemade tartar sauce, providing a true taste of Alaska. Beer drinkers are wont to accompany their buttwich with a selection from more than forty brews on tap at Humpy's.

WHERE TO GO:

Humpy's Great Alaskan Alehouse
610 West 6th Avenue
Anchorage, AK 99501
(907) 276-BEER [2337]
www.humpys.com

BILL'S WAY HALIBUT BURGER

Reprinted with permission from Humpy's Great Alaskan
Alehouse, Anchorage, Alaska

FOR EACH SANDWICH:

Olive oil

1 (5-ounce) halibut fillet

1 slice cheddar cheese

1 ounce thinly sliced bell pepper, sautéed

1 ounce thinly sliced white onion,
   sautéed

1 hamburger bun

3/4-ounce thick salsa, drained
   of excess juice

Lettuce

Thinly sliced tomato

Tartar sauce (see page 104)

PREHEAT A GRILL and brush it lightly with olive oil to avoid sticking. Grill the halibut fillet about 2 $1/2$ minutes per side, or until it just flakes easily with a fork. While grilling the second side of the halibut, top it with the cheddar cheese, pepper, and onion. The cheese should be melted by the time the fish is done, but if not, cover it and cook for a minute longer. Place the halibut on the bottom half of the bun and top it with the salsa, lettuce, and tomato. Spread the top half of the bun with tartar sauce, and place atop the halibut burger. Serve immediately.

Yield: 1 sandwich

ARIZONA

Monument Valley, stretching through northeastern Arizona and southeastern Utah, is the official land of the Navajo and Hopi Indians. The giant reservation is characterized by towering orange and red sandstone monoliths and buttes that stand in stark contrast to the flatness of the vast desert floor beneath them. Visitors from throughout the world come to view this beautiful land, made famous in Westerns directed by John Ford that often starred actor John Wayne.

The Navajos, who call themselves Diné (the People), likely arrived in the region between 500 and 700 years ago. Contact with white explorers and settlers had a lasting impact on their foodways. Sheep and herding brought mutton, a dietary meat staple, and wheat flour was eventually introduced. The latter was used to make fry bread, which is a round slab of dough about ten inches across and an inch thick that's fried one side at a time. Food historians believe that the preparation of fry bread, called **dah díníilghaazh** by the Navajo, began fifty to a hundred years ago. The Navajo taco, made from flavorful, flat fry bread layered with a variety of toppings similar to a tostada, is an adaptation from regional Arizona-Mexican cooking. It has become so popular that Arizona adopted it as the official state dish in 1995.

The Navajo taco is a specialty of the Stagecoach Dining Room at Goulding's Lodge, located adjacent to the Navajo Tribal Park in Monument Valley. Harry Goulding and his wife, "Mike," established it as a trading post in 1923. Today, Goulding's offers food and lodging as well as a museum and Navajo arts and crafts.

WHERE TO GO:

Goulding's Lodge and Tours
P.O. Box 360001
Monument Valley, UT 84536
(435) 727-3231
www.gouldings.com

NAVAJO FRY BREAD:

4 cups flour

1 tablespoon baking powder

1 teaspoon salt (optional)

1 1/4 cups warm water

2 cups lard or vegetable shortening

NAVAJO TACO:

1 piece of Navajo fry bread (see above)

6 to 8 ounces of chili con carne, with or without beans (Goulding's recommends Chefmate brand), or use Mexican chili beans for a vegetarian version

Grated cheddar cheese

Grated Monterey jack cheese

Chopped onion

Shredded lettuce

Chopped fresh tomatoes

Salsa

GOULDING'S LODGE NAVAJO TACOS

Reprinted with permission from Goulding's Lodge
and Tours, Monument Valley, Utah

MIX TOGETHER THE FLOUR, baking powder, and salt (optional). Add warm water a little at a time to form the dough, and knead until the dough is soft and not sticky. Place dough in a bowl, cover with a cloth, and let it stand for 1 hour.

When the dough is ready, divide and shape it into small balls about the size of a peach. Use cooking spray on your hands to prevent dough from sticking. Pat the dough back and forth by hand until it is about 8 inches in diameter and about $1/8$-inch thick. Make a small slit in the center of each round. Melt lard or shortening in a deep, heavy frying pan until smoking hot. Carefully put the rounds into hot fat, one at a time, and brown on both sides; the fry bread will puff up to approximately $1/4$ to $1/2$ inch thick. Drain the fry bread on paper towels before layering with the ingredients for the Navajo taco.

Yield: 9 pieces of fry bread

HEAT THE CHILI AND SPREAD it on a fresh, hot piece of fry bread. Top chili mixture with cheeses and onion to taste. Add a handful of lettuce, and garnish the top with tomatoes and a little more cheese. Serve with salsa on the side.

Yield: 1 Navajo taco

The phrase "chicken every Sunday" once signified a comfortable standard of living, if not wealth, sought by most Americans. But it wasn't until after World War II that chicken became affordable to people other than the most affluent. Today, chicken is not only affordable, but it has increased in popularity, leading all meats in per capita consumption at more than 80 pounds per year.

Folks in Arkansas are mighty partial to chicken, and it's no wonder. Arkansas ranks first among states in broiler production, accounting for some 15 percent of the national total. Chicken sandwiches are found on many restaurant menus throughout the state, and one of the best variations is that served at the Community Bakery Café in Little Rock, an establishment that has frequently been voted the number one bakery in the area. Patrons especially favor the fresh croissants filled with a delicious chicken tarragon salad topped with fresh tomato slices. Followed by a couple of Community Bakery's sugar cookies or a brownie, it's an addiction some customers just can't break.

WHERE TO GO:

Community Bakery Café
1200 Main Street
Little Rock, AR 72202
(501) 375-7105

Chicken Salad with Tarragon and Artichokes Sandwich

The tarragon chicken salad created by the late Bert Greene,
a well-known cookbook author, provided the inspiration for this version.

CHICKEN SALAD:

3 $\frac{1}{2}$ cups cooked chicken breast, cut into 1-inch cubes

1 $\frac{1}{4}$ cups quality mayonnaise

1 cup finely chopped celery

$\frac{1}{2}$ cup finely grated fresh carrot

$\frac{1}{2}$ cup finely chopped sweet red bell pepper

2 teaspoons dried tarragon

$\frac{1}{2}$ teaspoon dried oregano

Salt and freshly ground black pepper to taste

1 (14-ounce) can artichoke hearts packed in water, drained and coarsely chopped

COMBINE ALL INGREDIENTS for chicken salad. Cover and refrigerate at least 4 hours to allow flavors to blend.

SANDWICH:

6 white or whole wheat pocket pita breads, cut in half, or 12 fresh croissants

Lettuce

Chicken salad (see left)

Sweet red pepper strips (optional)

LINE EACH SIDE of the pita bread halves with a lettuce leaf. Fill pockets with chicken salad, and garnish with red pepper strips if desired. If using croissants, cut in half and place a lettuce leaf on the bottom slice; add chicken salad, top with red pepper strips if desired, cover with croissant top, and slice in half. Serve immediately.

Yield: 6 pita sandwiches or 12 croissant sandwiches

NOTE: 12 mini-pocket pita breads may be substituted for the large-size pita.

French emigrant Philippe Mathieu created the French Dip in 1918. This momentous event took place at his sandwich shop, Philippe the Original, which he established in 1908 in downtown Los Angeles. As the story goes, Philippe accidentally dropped a French roll into the roast pan drippings as he was making a sandwich for a hungry policeman. The policeman enjoyed the result so much that he soon returned with several friends in tow, all requesting that their sandwiches be "dipped" as well.

According to the current owners of Philippe the Original, it is not known if the now-famous sandwich was named the "French Dip" because of the French roll used to make the sandwich, because of Philippe's French heritage, or because the police officer's last name was French.

Over 5,000 people per day visit Philippe's in search of an authentic French Dip. With sawdust-strewn floors, the restaurant retains much of the character of its earlier years. While most people associate the French Dip sandwich with roast beef, today's specialty at Philippe the Original can be ordered with roast beef, roast pork, leg of lamb, baked ham, or roast turkey, all served on a French roll that has been dipped in natural gravy resulting from roasting the meat. Sandwiches at Philippe's can be ordered single- or double-dipped, and the restaurant offers a special hot-mustard sauce as an option.

The following recipe is based on the roasting method for beef supplied by Pat Bruno for his Chicago Italian Beef sandwiches, which were derived, according to legend, from the French Dip sandwich.

FOR EACH SANDWICH:

1 (4-pound) sirloin tip beef roast, trimmed of excess fat

Ground black pepper

1 cup beef stock

1 1/2 cups cold beef stock

1 teaspoon liquid garlic

5 to 6 French bread rolls or 6-inch lengths of French bread

WHERE TO GO:

Philippe the Original
1001 North Alameda Street
Los Angeles, California 90012
(213) 628-3781
www.philippes.com

THE FRENCH DIP

PREHEAT OVEN to 475 degrees. Sprinkle roast all over with plenty of ground black pepper, pressing it into the meat as much as possible. Place meat in a small roasting pan, and add the 1 cup of beef stock. Roast the beef at 475 degrees for 35 minutes, then reduce the oven temperature to 400 degrees and roast for 40 minutes. Do not turn off the oven.

Remove roast from oven and pour the $1^1/2$ cups cold beef stock into the bottom of the roasting pan. Let stand 15 to 20 minutes. Add garlic juice to broth in bottom of pan, and return the roast to the oven. Roast until meat reaches the desired degree of doneness for rare or medium; test with a meat thermometer. (Some people like their beef for French dip well done and falling into pieces while others prefer medium-rare to medium beef.)

Remove pan from oven and set roast on a platter or caving board to cool slightly before carving. Transfer the au jus to a small, wide pan and keep it warm over low heat.

Cut the rolls or bread open horizontally and, if desired, remove some of the bread from the inside, creating a pocket to hold the beef. Slice beef as thinly as possible. Dip rolls quickly into the au jus, fill generously with sliced beef, and serve immediately.

Yield: 5 to 6 sandwiches

NOTE: Garlic juice is available in liquid form or spray bottles from gourmet food shops. If using garlic spray, note that 8 spritzes are equal to 1 teaspoon liquid garlic or 1 clove of garlic.

DENVER SANDWICH

Reprinted with permission from the Durango Diner, Durango, Colorado

OMELET FILLING:

1 1/2 tablespoons butter

1 1/2 tablespoons chopped green bell pepper

2 tablespoons chopped onion

1/4 cup cubed ham

1/4 cup coarsely chopped fresh tomato

IN A SMALL FRYING PAN, melt butter over medium heat. Add green pepper, onion, and ham, and sauté until vegetables are tender. Remove from heat, add chopped tomato, and set aside in a warm place.

KITCHEN SINK OMELET:

3 eggs

1 tablespoon water or milk

1 tablespoon butter

Omelet filling (see left)

1 thin slice American cheese

1 thin slice Swiss cheese

1/4 cup grated sharp Cheddar cheese

IN A SMALL BOWL, beat the eggs with the water or milk. In a medium frying pan or 8-inch omelet pan, melt butter over medium heat. Add the egg mixture followed by the vegetable and ham mixture; cook the omelet by tilting the pan and care-fully lifting the edges of the omelet in order to cook all of the egg without turning the omelet over. When omelet is partially cooked, top with the cheeses and fold the other side over. Continue cooking just long enough to melt the cheese.

Yield: 1 omelet

SANDWICH:

2 Kitchen Sink Omelets (see left)

6 slices white, rye, or whole wheat bread, toasted and buttered

Salt and pepper to taste

Divide the 2 omelets among 3 slices of the buttered toast, add salt and pepper to taste, and top each with another slice of toast. Cut sandwiches in half and serve immediately.

Yield: 3 sandwiches

WHERE TO GO:

Durango Diner
957 Main Avenue
Durango, CO 81301
(970) 247-9889
www.durangodiner.com

There are several theories relative to the origin of the Denver sandwich. The first states that pioneers created it on the long trek West as a way to disguise the taste of eggs that had gone bad. Supposedly, the eggs were mixed with onion and other seasonings that might have been at hand. One wonders about this theory since most wagons, too heavily loaded to begin with, had to ditch valuable provisions early on. Eggs would have necessarily been cradled in straw or hay to prevent breakage and packed in heavy barrels designed to endure transport over barely recognizable trails. Surely, they would have been among the first provisions to be discarded. A second theory proposes that chuck-wagon cooks may have invented the Denver sandwich to be carried as a snack in cowboy's saddlebags. Finally, a third theory says the Denver sandwich was invented by Chinese cooks attempting to Americanize egg foo yung. In **American Cookery,** James Beard states that the Denver sandwich originated with Chinese cooks who manned the stoves for logging camps and rail-road gangs in the nineteenth and early twentieth centuries.

The first identified print reference to date is from a 1918 restaurant industry publication. Quite possibly, the development of the Denver sandwich paralleled that of the St. Paul sandwich (see page 73), with both devised by enterprising Chinese cooks anxious to adapt their cooking to American foods and tastes. The basic Denver sandwich is composed of an omelet made with diced ham, onion, and green pepper. It's typically served on buttered toast made from white, rye, or whole wheat bread. In diner lingo, the Denver became known as a Western and both are called a Cowboy.

In the old mining town of Durango, Colorado, hungry folks flock to the landmark Durango Diner, known far and wide for its great breakfasts. Here, the classic Denver omelet has been updated to include both tomatoes and cheese, is topped with the diner's green chili or sausage gravy, and has been given a new name: the Kitchen Sink Omelet. The latter isn't served as a sandwich but is presented with the addition of that delicious chili and a side of Colorado hash browns, which no one seems to mind. Owners Gary and Donna Broad sell Durango Diner Green Chili and other products by mail.

Bob Cobb, manager of the legendary Brown Derby Restaurants in California, created the Cobb Salad shortly after the opening of the first location in Hollywood in 1926. The salad rapidly became one of the establishment's signature dishes, and although the Brown Derby Restaurants are now closed, Cobb Salad has never lost its popularity.

Wraps became trendy in the 1990s, creating a new benchmark for the American sandwich. According to Lori Lyn Narlock, coauthor of **Wraps,** they originated in San Francisco and Northern California. The concept was based on the enhancement and glamorization of the burrito, a long-established favorite throughout California and the American Southwest. Usually starting with a flour tortilla (but sometimes making use of flatbread), a variety of fillings are combined in imaginative pairings and laid on the tortilla, which is folded in at one or both ends, then rolled up from one edge of the tortilla.

Wraps were so well received in restaurants and takeout shops that it wasn't long before they spread across the country and began appearing in airports and supermarket snack shops, offering yet another alternative to the demand for food-on-the-run. While industry experts say the wrap never really caught on in the Southwest and that the wrap trend may have met its demise in California, they continue to be popular throughout many parts of the country.

At the historic Tavern on Main (circa 1810) in upscale Westport, Connecticut, Executive Chef David Raymer pays tribute to American culinary tradition by including a Rolled Cobb Sandwich that incorporates the wrap trend. Raymer's trendy luncheon menu also includes several innovative versions of New England specialties like the Grilled Grafton Cheddar, Tomato, and Maple-Smoked Bacon Sandwich, and the Warm New England Lobster Roll. Chef Raymer's dressing for the Rolled Cobb Sandwich is so delicious that you'll want to regularly serve it on a variety of salads.

ROLLED COBB SANDWICH

Reprinted with permission from Chef David Raymer, Tavern on Main, Westport, Connecticut

DRESSING:

3 egg yolks

1 tablespoon Dijon mustard

$1/2$ cup red wine vinegar

Juice of 1 lemon

2 $1/2$ cups pure olive oil

Kosher salt

Freshly ground black pepper

IN A MEDIUM BOWL, whisk the egg yolks with the mustard. Whisk in the wine vinegar and the lemon juice until well incorporated. Whisking constantly, slowly drizzle in the olive oil to form an emulsion. Season to taste with salt and pepper. If preferred, this dressing can be easily made in a food processor.

Yield: about 3 $1/2$ cups dressing or enough for approximately 12 sandwiches

SANDWICH:

1 lavash (a very thin, soft flatbread), lightly heated on a grill or in a toaster oven

Mesclun greens, chopped

Crumbled blue cheese (high quality, such as Maytag)

Turkey breast, diced

Avocado, diced

Fresh tomato, seeded, drained, and diced

Bacon, cooked crisp, drained, and diced

Hard-boiled egg, diced

Dressing (see left)

LAY THE LAVASH FLAT and sprinkle evenly and to taste with the mesclun greens, blue cheese, turkey, avocado, tomato, bacon, and hard-boiled egg. Drizzle with dressing. Roll up the lavash, slice in half on the diagonal, and serve immediately.

Yield: 1 sandwich

NOTE: Packaged smoked turkey breast topped with crushed black pepper is excellent in this sandwich. If lavash isn't available, substitute sun-dried tomato or another flavor wrap.

WHERE TO GO:

Tavern on Main
146 Main Street
Westport, CT 06880
(203) 221-7222
www.tavernonmain.com

A 31584 State Street Bridge, Westport, Conn.

While roast turkey may be the centerpiece of our traditional American Thanksgiving dinner, there are plenty of people who confess to a preference for leftovers from the big feast—especially turkey sandwiches. According to the National Turkey Federation, the number-one way to use Thanksgiving leftover turkey is in sandwiches.

Folks in Delaware are especially proud of a particular turkey sandwich and the one-woman success story behind it. Back in 1976, Lois Margolet decided to strike out on her own by opening a sandwich shop in the Little Italy section of Wilmington, Delaware. She named it Capriotti's, after her grandfather who taught her how to cook, and Lois and her brother, Alan Margolet, devoted long hours to the new endeavor. Lois created Capriotti's signature sandwich, The Bobbie®, which was named for her Aunt Bobbie Capriotti. After ten years of hard work, Capriotti's sandwiches were voted "Best in the State" by **Delaware Today** magazine, and business boomed.

Although Capriotti's now has several franchise operations in thirty-two locations throughout seven states, Lois and her family are still at the helm, ensuring that quality is maintained in both product and service. At the shops in Las Vegas, loyal Delaware patrons who produce their driver's licenses are rewarded with a free sub. At all their locations, Capriotti's has customers lined up for The Bobbie, which fans refer to as "Thanksgiving on a roll." Alan Margolet says the real secret to a great sandwich is the freshness of the turkey and the stuffing.

WHERE TO GO:

Capriotti's (the original shop in Little Italy)
501 North Union Street
Wilmington, DE 19805
(302) 571-8929

Additional locations are listed on Capriotti's web site at www.capriottis.com.

THE BOBBIE®

Reprinted with permission from Al-Lomar, Inc., Wilmington, Delaware

1 (9-inch) freshly baked sub roll

Mayonnaise

4 ounces thinly sliced freshly roasted turkey

4 ounces fresh turkey stuffing of choice

2 ounces cranberry sauce

Salt and pepper to taste

SPLIT THE SUB ROLL lengthwise and spread a light coating of mayonnaise on each half. On the bottom half of the roll, layer the turkey, stuffing, and cranberry sauce, and salt and pepper to taste. Cover with top of roll, slice in half, and serve immediately.

Yield: 1 sandwich

NOTE: Alan Margolet reports that some customers like to microwave The Bobbie for about 1 minute just before it's served.

May glad Thanksgivings Crown your days and years.

It is generally agreed that Cuban cigar workers who migrated to the Tampa, Florida, area around 1900 brought the Cuban sandwich to the United States. Enterprising Cubans established cigar factories at Ybor City, a few miles east of Tampa, and it soon became known as "Little Havana."

Originally known as the "mixto," or mixed sandwich, the Cuban, as it's called today, became a workingman's lunch for those employed in the Tampa cigar industry with little time to eat. The sandwiches were carried to work secured by toothpicks, and rapidly became a status symbol—after all, not everyone could afford to eat, and those who could, returned to work with a toothpick in their teeth.

According to food historian Andy Huse, those first Cuban emigrants in Ybor City were quite innovative when it came to re-creating their favorite sandwich from back home. They often used tailor's irons to press and glaze the sugar coating into their hams, and they also used the irons to press and grill their sandwiches.

Authentic crusty Cuban bread is considered crucial to a good sandwich, and it, too, has a history. According to Steve Otto of the **Tampa Tribune,** Cuban bread got its long, thin shape due to a flour shortage in Cuba at the time of the revolution of 1875. The bread is baked with palmetto leaves inserted along the top of the formed loaf, creating the distinct split crust. Otto also reports that in the old days, Ybor City bakers provided home delivery, impaling the loaves of bread onto nails that customers hammered next to their front doors. In **The Florida Cookbook,** authors Jeanne Voltz and Caroline Stuart report that bakeries were among the first businesses established by Cubans fleeing their homeland in 1959 and 1960. Loaves of Cuban bread are traditionally made in 36-inch lengths and are thus sometimes called "yard bread."

While most of the old cigar factories are now closed, Ybor City is a historical section of Tampa with the entire area a veritable bastion of great Cuban food. Although Tampa may claim title to the establishment of the Cuban sandwich cult in Florida, Miami is by no means left behind. There are dozens of great places to enjoy the sandwich there as well. The Cuban rules as the favorite sandwich among Floridians, with tens of thousands sold daily, and its popularity is spreading throughout the country.

Authentic Cuban sandwiches are based on crusty Cuban bread, similar to French bread but flatter and a bit drier. They are composed of thin slices of sugar-cured ham (preferably imported from Spain), thinly sliced and slowly roasted pork that has been bathed in mojo (a marinade of sour orange juice, oil, salt, oregano, garlic, and peppers), Swiss cheese, and thin slices of sour or dill pickle. Most diners request the optional mustard.

Additions like Genoa salami (contributed by Italian immigrants), mayonnaise, lettuce, tomato, and onion have become popular in the past forty years but are considered heresy by those who insist on authenticity and who follow the old way of just spreading on a bit of butter inside and out. In the old days, the sandwich was brushed on the outside with a small amount of pork drippings. Once assembled, the Cuban is placed in a sandwich press that compresses the sandwich while melting the cheese and heating the meats.

In searching for the definitive Cuban sandwich recipe for home use, we discovered an excellent web site that serves as a guide to just about everything Cuban, including food. Billing themselves as Three Guys From Miami, Raúl Musibay, Glenn Lindgren, and Jorge Castillo host iCuban.com: The Internet Cuban, generously sharing their considerable knowledge that's spiced with plenty of humor, travel recommendations, terrific recipes, and much more. They've even written a cookbook called **Three Guys From Miami Cook Cuban,** that's not to be missed by anyone interested in great Cuban cooking.

CUBAN SANDWICH

Recipe courtesy of Three Guys From Miami™;
iCuban.com: The Internet Cuban™ at http://icuban.com

ROAST PORK:

3 cloves garlic

1 teaspoon salt

1 tablespoon dried oregano

1 cup minced onion

1 cup sour orange juice (or use substitute recommended in Note below)

1/2 cup Spanish olive oil

1 (2-pound) boneless center-cut pork loin roast

MASH THE GARLIC and salt together with a mortar and pestle. (If you don't have a mortar and pestle, use a rolling pin and a cutting board.) Place the mixture in a small bowl. Add oregano, onion, and the sour orange juice to the mash and mix thoroughly. Heat oil in a small saucepan over medium heat, add the mash to the oil, and whisk the mixture together. Remove from heat and set the marinade aside.

Thoroughly pierce the pork roast with a sharp knife or fork. Set aside a small amount of the marinade for use during the roasting period. Pour remaining marinade over the pork, cover, and refrigerate for 2 to 3 hours.

Preheat oven to 325 degrees. Remove pork from refrigerator and place it on a rack in a roasting pan. Sprinkle remaining marinade over pork. Roast until completely cooked and a meat thermometer registers 160 degrees, about 20 minutes per pound. Baste occasionally with the pan juices. Remove pork from oven and let it rest for at least 20 minutes before thinly slicing the meat.

Bring remaining pan juices to a boil and simmer until juice is reduced by half. Use this juice to sprinkle onto the meat in the sandwiches.

NOTE: If you can't get sour oranges in your area, try equal parts of orange and grapefruit juices, or 2 parts orange juice to 1 part lemon juice and 1 part lime juice.

CUBAN SANDWICH:

Cuban bread (or substitute French bread if you must, but not a baguette)

Butter, softened

Sliced dill pickles

1 pound thinly sliced roasted Cuban pork (see page 29)

1 pound thinly sliced good-quality ham

1/2 pound thinly sliced mild Swiss cheese

Yellow mustard (optional)

Mayonnaise (optional)

Cooking spray

NEED A QUICK FIX?

Go to iCuban.com: The Internet Cuban™ for everything you could possibly need when it comes to Cuban recipes, fresh Cuban or *medianoche* bread, Cuban sandwich presses, mojo marinades, and several thousand other Cuban specialty items. Orders are placed quickly via the Internet, and in no time at all, you'll be reproducing an authentic taste of Cuba right in your own home. Here's the web site: http://icuban.com

CUT THE BREAD into four sections, each about 8 inches long. Slice these in half horizontally and spread butter on the inside of both halves. Generously layer sandwiches with filling ingredients in the following order: pickles, roasted pork, ham, and cheese. Spread with the optional mustard or mayonnaise if desired.

Preheat a pancake griddle or a large frying pan. Lightly coat the hot griddle or frying pan with cooking spray and add the first sandwich. (Make sure that your griddle or frying pan is not too hot or the crust will burn before the cheese melts.) Place a heavy iron skillet or bacon press on top of the sandwich to flatten it. (You really want to smash the sandwich, compressing the bread to about a third of its original size.) Grill the sandwich for 2 to 3 minutes on each side, until the cheese is melted and the bread is golden. Repeat process for remaining sandwiches. Slice each sandwich in half diagonally and serve.

Yield: 4 generous sandwiches

MEDIANOCHE SANDWICH

THE MEDIANOCHE is the "sister sandwich" to the Cuban, and its name translates to "midnight"—apparently because it's eaten in the early hours of the morning after a night on the town. The difference between the two is in the bread: the medianoche is made on a smaller Cuban egg roll that is sweeter in taste, similar to challah.

For medianoche sandwiches, use all the same ingredients as listed for the Cuban sandwich, except substitute a medianoche bread loaf. The sweeter bread and smaller size are the only difference between a medianoche and a Cuban sandwich!

NOTES FROM THREE GUYS FROM MIAMI:

Bring the meats and cheese to room temperature before making the sandwiches. This will help you avoid burning the bread, and the cheese will melt perfectly. This is especially helpful if you put a lot of meat in the sandwiches.

Serrano ham, a dry, slightly salty ham similar to Italian prosciutto, is great for Cuban sandwiches and makes a very tasty addition.

For extra flavor, sprinkle a little mojo or meat juice on the pork and ham before adding the cheese.

Using mustard or mayonnaise is a personal choice. We find that the best Cuban sandwiches don't need either ingredient. The butter, natural meat juices, and yes, even the pickle juice, give it all the moistness and flavor it needs. At lunch counters we've seen many people dipping their sandwich into a little mustard, so it's perfectly acceptable to serve it as a side condiment.

WHERE TO GO:

In Miami, Florida, the Three Guys From Miami recommend the Latin American Cafeteria. A local chain, it's basically a mom-and-pop-type operation with atmosphere typical of Miami's Cuban lunch counters. Skip the outdoor take-out window and go inside where you'll see Cuban sandwiches made to order, or sit at the counter and soak up the attention of the friendly waitresses. Often recommended is the following location:

Latin American Cafeteria
401 Biscayne Boulevard
Miami, FL 33132
(305) 387-7774

Tampa, Florida, has plenty of places to get great Cuban sandwiches, including:

La Teresita
3248 West Columbus Drive
Tampa, FL 33607
(813) 879-9704

Pimiento cheese is a favorite sandwich filling and specialty of the American South, where it is referred to as "Southern comfort food." In Georgia, where it's especially popular, pimiento cheese is purchased off grocery shelves or, more likely, made fresh at home. Georgia, by the way, is the leading grower of pimiento peppers in the United States.

As early as 1910, **The Washington Post** carried advertisements for pimiento cheese. Mrs. S. R. Dull provided a recipe for Open Pimiento Toast in **Southern Cooking,** originally published in 1928. Mrs. Dull was a well-known food authority in her day, having worked for the **Atlanta Journal** as editor of the Home Economics page, and she was referred to as "The first lady of cooking in Georgia and the outstanding culinary expert of the South." Her recipe instructs the cook to trim the crusts from whole wheat bread and toast it. Butter and pimiento cheese are spread on the toast, the slice is cut into three pieces, and then placed in a hot oven until the cheese begins to melt. She advocates serving the toast with coffee, commenting that it is "nice for a last course at dinner." This dainty savory was most likely the precursor of the hearty pimiento cheese sandwich that became popular during the Depression.

While no one has yet discovered the true origin of pimiento cheese, many Southern food writers quote author Reynolds Price, whose comments appeared in the 1981 **Great American Writers' Cookbook.** Price notes his failure in an extensive effort to discover its origin, but he does recall it as "the peanut butter of his childhood," homemade by his mother. Price was born in 1933 in Macon, North Carolina, indicating that pimiento cheese was undoubtedly a well-established food by then. In today's South, pimiento cheese is just as likely to make its appearance as a topping on hot dogs and hamburgers as a filling for sandwiches. There are probably as many variations of pimiento cheese as cooks, with suggested additions including mustard, hot red pepper sauce, chopped green onion, garlic, lemon juice, horseradish, wine, or Worcestershire sauce.

As for Georgia restaurants that serve great P. C. sandwiches, the hands-down winner is Vera's Café in Augusta, Georgia, operated by Vera Stewart, whose mail-order gourmet food business, Very Vera, has reached epic proportions. With its enamel-topped, old-fashioned tables and black-and-white-tiled floors, the café is reminiscent of a vintage 1950s eatery. One of Vera's signature sandwiches is grilled pimiento cheese, bacon, and tomato on marble rye bread (the other is her delicious chicken salad). Of course, no one can resist Vera's famous cakes—ordered by the slice for dessert or, more likely, by taking an entire cake home—which her grandmother, Vera Wingfield of Atlanta, taught her to make as a young girl. Visitors who may somehow have missed Vera's Café in town can still grab a P. C. sandwich and other goodies-to-go at her new satellite location in the Augusta International Airport.

WHERE TO GO:

Vera's Café
3113 Washington Road
Augusta, GA 30907
(706) 860-3492
(800) 500-VERA [8372] toll free
www.veryvera.com

Also located at the Augusta International Airport

NEED A QUICK FIX?

Very Vera's homemade pimiento cheese is available by the pound for take-out. Special requests for mail-order shipment are accommodated during cool months of the year.

"THE GRILL" PIMIENTO CHEESE SANDWICH

Reprinted with permission from Vera Stewart, owner and creator of
Very Vera's and Vera's Café, Augusta, Georgia

NOTE: Vera's recipe for pimiento cheese, made from scratch with freshly ground pimiento, is a carefully guarded secret. If you find yourself without Vera's P. C., try the following:

PIMIENTO CHEESE:

10 ounces quality sharp cheddar cheese, grated

1 (4-ounce) jar pimientos, drained

1/2 cup mayonnaise

1 tablespoon lemon juice

1 teaspoon Worcestershire sauce

1/8 teaspoon cayenne pepper (or more, to taste)

COMBINE ALL INGREDIENTS in a mixing bowl. Mix well with a fork, mashing the mixture a bit to create a chunky-style spread. Store in a tightly covered container and refrigerate for several hours or overnight, allowing flavors to blend.

Yield: 2 cups

VERA'S P.C. SANDWICH:

2 slices of marble rye bread (a combination of dark and light rye bread)

Butter

1/4 cup pimiento cheese (see left)

2 medium-thick slices of tomato

2 slices bacon, cooked crisp and drained

BUTTER ONE SIDE of each slice of bread. Spread one slice with pimiento cheese and lay buttered side down in a frying pan. Add the tomato and bacon and cover the sandwich with the remaining slice of bread, buttered side up. Over medium heat, grill the sandwich until golden brown on both sides, watching it carefully so that it doesn't burn. Remove sandwich from pan, slice in half, and serve immediately.

Yield: 1 sandwich

GRILLED HAWAIIAN AHI WITH APPLEWOOD-SMOKED BACON SANDWICH

Reprinted with permission from Mama's Fish House, Paia, Maui, Hawaii

MAUI ONION RANCH-STYLE DRESSING:

1 tablespoon minced garlic

1/4 cup finely chopped Maui onion (or substitute another sweet onion such as Vidalia)

1 teaspoon sugar

1 teaspoon dry mustard

1 teaspoon chopped fresh thyme

1 teaspoon Worcestershire sauce

2 tablespoons red wine vinegar

1/4 cup regular pure olive oil (not extra virgin)

1 cup quality mayonnaise

Salt and freshly ground black pepper, to taste

PLACE ALL INGREDIENTS in a medium bowl, mix well, cover, and chill in the refrigerator.

FRUIT SALAD:

1 cup diced fresh pineapple

1 cup diced fresh banana

1 cup diced fresh mango

Juice of 1 fresh lime

1 teaspoon honey

2 fresh mint leaves, chopped

PLACE ALL ingredients in a medium bowl, mix well, cover, and chill in the refrigerator.

WHERE TO GO:

Mama's Fish House
799 Poho Place
Paia, Maui, HI 96779
(808) 579-8488
www.mamasfishhouse.com

NEED A QUICK FIX?

Applewood-smoked bacon, produced by Niman Ranch, is sold in quality markets nationwide or via mail order at www.nimanranch.com.

SANDWICH:

4 (4- to 5-ounce) fresh ahi fillets

Salt and freshly ground black pepper, to taste

4 pieces focaccia bread, sliced and toasted

Maui Onion Ranch-Style Dressing (see left)

Butter lettuce

Lolla rosa (red leaf) lettuce

Kula tomato slices (or substitute another
   variety of fresh, quality tomato)

12 strips applewood-smoked bacon, fried crisp
   and drained

Yield: 4 sandwiches

SEASON THE AHI FILLETS with salt and pepper to taste, then grill the fillets to the desired temperature and degree of doneness; it is suggested that they be cooked no more than medium. Spread all slices of the toasted focaccia bread with the dressing. On each of four slices of focaccia, layer a cooked ahi fillet, butter lettuce, lolla rosa lettuce, sliced tomato, and 3 strips of bacon. Top each sandwich with the remaining focaccia halves, slice the sandwiches in half, and serve accompanied by the fruit salad. At Mama's Fish House, Molokai sweet-potato chips are also served with the sandwich.

Visitors flock to Hawaii for any number of reasons, including deep-sea fishing, or at least enjoying the ocean's bounty at the dining table. One of the most popular of Hawaiian fish is the ahi, or yellowfin tuna, a hard-fighting heavyweight. It provides a challenge to fishermen but is the darling of the area's restaurant chefs due to its versatility and ease of preparation. Ahi provides the basis for many delectable dinner entrees, and it's also featured in delightful luncheon sandwiches that provide tasty, lingering memories for tourists to Hawaii.

There's no better ahi sandwich than that served at Mama's Fish House in Paia on the island of Maui. Floyd and Doris Christenson established Mama's in 1973. Located right on the beach with spectacular ocean views, fresh fish is the byword at Mama's, and while their menu has been continually updated to reflect changing tastes and exciting new ingredients, the longevity of the staff is a testimony to the Christensons' dedication to consistent quality and service. Mike Pascher has served as fish cutter for twenty-five years, while Perry Bateman has been executive chef for fifteen years. Chef Geoff Martin created the fabulous grilled ahi sandwich served at Mama's, along with a delightful fresh fruit salad, and it's one of the most popular items on the menu. It's served on sourdough focaccia bread made from an eight-year-old starter and then deliciously gussied up with the addition of herbs and cheddar cheese from the Grafton Village Cheese Company in Vermont (see page 124).

THE FISHING IS EXCELLENT HERE.

Greetings from Coeur d'Alene, Idaho

Trout and Ernest Hemingway are as synonymous with Idaho as potatoes. Hemingway, often called "a man's man" because of his passion for hunting and fishing, spent considerable time in Idaho, where he enjoyed fishing for both brown and rainbow trout on Silver Creek, near Ketchum and Sun Valley. In 1934, the State of Idaho constructed what would become only the first of many trout-rearing facilities, including those in Magic Valley. Today, the United States ranks second in world production of trout, with 70 to 75 percent of its total produced in Idaho.

Much of Idaho's trout production is used for the preparation of smoked trout. Hickey Foods, owned and operated by Tom and Lucy Hickey, specializes in the finest vacuum-packed smoked trout from Magic Valley trout farms, and they ship nationwide to both commercial customers and individual consumers. Smoked trout from Hickey Foods is a requisite for the delicious Sandwich de Amy served at Redfish Lake Lodge in Stanley, Idaho. Amy Poehling, whose father was an owner of the lodge for several years, created the sandwich. Located at the headwaters of the Salmon River's main fork and surrounded by the majestic beauty of Idaho's Sawtooth Mountains, Redfish Lake Lodge caters to discriminating palates and appetites sharpened by a full range of outdoor activities.

WHERE TO GO:

Redfish Lake Lodge (seasonal)
P.O. Box 9
Stanley, ID 83278
(208) 774-3536
www.redfishlake.com

NEED A QUICK FIX?

Smoked Idaho trout as well as smoked salmon can be ordered directly from:

Hickey Foods
P.O. Box 2312
Sun Valley, ID 83353
(208) 788-9033

SANDWICH DE AMY

Reprinted with permission from Redfish Lake Lodge, Stanley, Idaho

BECKY MERCURI'S PESTO:

2 cups fresh basil leaves, washed and dried on paper towels

1 teaspoon kosher salt

1 teaspoon freshly ground black pepper

2 large cloves garlic, finely chopped

1/2 cup quality extra-virgin olive oil

1/4 cup pine nuts (pignola nuts)

1/4 cup freshly grated Parmesan cheese

1/4 cup freshly grated Romano cheese

PLACE ALL INGREDIENTS except cheeses into a food processor and blend until smooth. Transfer mixture to a bowl and stir in the cheese. Before using, cover and refrigerate for 2 hours to let flavors blend.

Yield: 1 1/2 cups

SANDWICH:

1 (5- to 6-inch) length French bread, sliced crosswise in half

3 to 4 tablespoons pesto, to taste (see left)

1 (4-ounce) boneless fillet of ruby red smoked trout (Hickey Foods brand is recommended)

4 to 6 very thin slices Roma tomato

Freshly grated Parmesan cheese

Freshly ground black pepper

SPREAD FRENCH BREAD with pesto to taste. Slice the trout fillet in half lengthwise and place on top of pesto; top with tomato slices, sprinkle lightly with freshly grated Parmesan, and season to taste with freshly ground black pepper. Serve as an open-faced sandwich.

Yield: 1 sandwich

Our search for the origin of the Italian beef sandwich led directly to Pasquale "Pat" Bruno, dining critic for the Chicago **Sun-Times,** cookbook author, and an expert on foods of the Windy City.

During the 1890s, Italian emigrants poured into Chicago's Near West Side, bordered by Polk and Taylor Streets, and by the 1920s, Italians made up the area's largest ethnic group. While stories and claims abound as to who should be rightfully credited for Italian beef, Bruno cuts straight to the chase, stating that it's clearly a descendant of the French Dip sandwich that dates back to 1918 in Los Angeles. He points out that expensive cuts of beef were definitely not a staple of Italian kitchens during the Depression years or even before, and it remained rare in most Italian households right through the 1950s, thus pretty much discrediting earlier claims to the origin of the sandwich.

Bruno is inclined to believe one legend, which says an Italian cook named Tony, who worked in a Greek coffee shop around 1948 or 1949, created the sandwich. Thinking the French Dip served in that establishment was pretty bland, Tony threw in some garlic and herbs, a move that earned him accolades from just about everyone but the owner, who fired him on the spot. Undaunted, Tony opened a successful Italian beef stand down the street and the rest is history.

The basis of the Italian beef sandwich, a Chicago favorite, is very thinly sliced roast beef that has been seasoned with Italian herbs and spices. The beef slices are dipped in the thin, Italian-style gravy (actually an au jus created from the roasting process), highly flavored with garlic, ground black pepper, crushed red pepper, basil, and oregano. The beef is then placed onto a crusty roll (that may or may not also be dipped in the gravy), and topped with giardiniera, an Italian relish composed of finely chopped vegetables like hot peppers, celery, carrots, and spices in olive oil. More sweet or hot peppers may top it off. A "combo" sandwich calls for the addition of a grilled Italian sausage.

Because many beef stands offer only counter eating, fans have developed the famous "Chicago lean," described by Pat Bruno as follows: "feet spread about as wide as your shoulders, elbows on the counter, lean forward as you bite."

From his book **Chicago Food Favorites: A Guide to More Than 450 Favorite Eating Spots** (now out of print), Pat Bruno also shares instructions on just how to order an Italian beef sandwich:

- "Beef. Dry, sweet." Beef sandwich with sweet peppers and a little less gravy.
- "Beef. Wet, hot." Beef sandwich with hot peppers and a lot of gravy (the roll is soaked with gravy before the beef is loaded into the roll).
- "Beef. Dry, hot." The same as the first one only with hot peppers instead of sweet.
- "Combo." Half beef and half Italian sausage.

PAT BRUNO'S ITALIAN BEEF SANDWICH

Reprinted with permission from Pasquale "Pat" Bruno Jr., dining critic for the Chicago *Sun-Times* and author of *The Great Chicago-Style Pizza Cookbook* and *Pasta Tecnica*

CHICAGO-STYLE GIARDINIERA

(Italian hot pepper relish)

1/4 cup coarsely chopped carrots

1/4 cup 1/8-inch-thick slices sport peppers, sliced on the bias

1/4 cup very small cauliflower florets

3/4 cup 1/8-inch-thick slices celery, sliced on the bias

1/4 to 1/2 cup sliced jalapeños, as desired, for mild or hot flavor

1 teaspoon dried oregano, crumbled

1/2 teaspoon finely chopped garlic

2/3 cup olive oil

2 tablespoons white wine vinegar

IN A NONREACTIVE BOWL or container, combine all the vegetables with the oregano and garlic. Add the oil and vinegar, and toss to combine. Cover and store in a cool place, but do not refrigerate. Giardiniera should be made at least 1 day ahead of use to allow flavors to infuse. Serve as a topping for Italian beef sandwiches. The amount used on each sandwich varies according to taste, but approximately 3 generous tablespoons per sandwich works just fine.

Yield: 2 1/2 cups

NOTE: Sport peppers are a Chicago favorite, and they are served on everything from classic Chicago hot dogs to Italian beef sandwiches. Once known as the Mississippi sport pepper, they belong to the serrano chile family, and most of them are now imported from Mexico. Look for sport peppers, sold in jars, in the condiment section of the supermarket. Crushed red pepper flakes may be substituted for the jalapeños. If desired, vegetable oil may be substituted for olive oil.

SPICE RUB:

1 teaspoon dried basil

1 teaspoon dried oregano

1 teaspoon garlic powder

1 teaspoon ground black pepper

1 teaspoon salt

1 teaspoon red pepper flakes

MAKE A SPICE RUB by combining the basil, oregano, garlic powder, ground black pepper, salt, and red pepper flakes.

ROAST BEEF:

1 (4-pound) sirloin tip beef roast, trimmed of excess fat

Spice rub (see above)

1 cup water

1 1/2 cups cold water

2 to 3 teaspoons garlic juice (optional), to taste

PREHEAT OVEN to 475 degrees. Rub half of the spice rub over and around the beef roast.

Press the mixture into the meat as much as possible. Place the meat in a roasting pan and add the cup of water to the bottom of the pan; add more if necessary to cover entire bottom of pan. Roast the beef at 475 degrees for 35 minutes. Reduce the temperature to 400 degrees and roast for 40 minutes. Do not turn off the oven.

Remove beef from oven and pour the cold water into the bottom of the pan. Let stand 15 to 20 minutes. Add remaining seasoning mixture and garlic juice (optional) to the pan juices and water. Return meat to the oven and roast until a meat thermometer registers 160 degrees, about 50 minutes. Note that because oven temperatures vary, the use of a meat thermometer is important.

Remove pan from oven and allow meat to stand and cool somewhat before slicing. Slice beef almost paper-thin; the right thinness is critical to ensure a good chew but without toughness.

Transfer the juices to a saucepan and keep warm over low heat. Immerse the sliced beef into the warm gravy.

SANDWICH:

Sliced roast beef (see left)

8 to 10 French or Italian bread rolls, 6 inches in length

Chicago-style giardiniera (see page 39)

Chopped green bell peppers, grilled in olive oil (optional)

TO SERVE, scoop about $^1/4$ to $^1/3$ pound of beef out of the gravy with a fork. Load it into a French or Italian bread roll. Garnish with giardiniera or grilled green bell peppers.

Yield: 8 to 10 sandwiches

PAT'S NOTES: One of the secrets used by Chicago Italian beef stands is the addition of garlic juice to the pan juices during the final roasting. Garlic juice is available in liquid form or spray bottles from gourmet food shops. It does add immensely to the flavor. If using garlic spray, note that 8 spritzes are equal to 1 teaspoon of liquid garlic or one clove of garlic.

It is not the custom of Italian beef stands to undercook the beef. In fact, more often than not, the beef is roasted until it is what you might call "medium well," which means very little red is visible.

If you like a "wet" beef sandwich, dip the roll into the gravy before loading in the sliced beef.

WHERE TO GO:

Mr. Beef
666 North Orleans Street
Chicago, IL 60610
(312) 337-8500

Al's # 1 Italian Beef
1079 West Taylor Street
Chicago, IL 60607
(312) 226-4017

Johnnie's Beef
7500 West North Avenue
Elmwood Park, IL 60707
(708) 452-6000

NEED A QUICK FIX?

Giardiniera and sport peppers can be ordered from:

Vincent Formusa Company
710 West Grand Avenue
Chicago, IL 60610
(312) 421-0485

Hot giardiniera can be ordered from:

The Vermont Country Store
www.vermontcountrystore.com

MIDWESTERN PORK TENDERLOIN SANDWICH

Reprinted with permission from www.otherwhitemeat.com and the National Pork Board

PORK:

1 pound boneless pork loin

1 cup flour

1 teaspoon salt

1/2 teaspoon ground black pepper

CUT 4 (1-INCH-THICK) SLICES of pork. Trim any exterior fat from edges. Put each slice of pork between pieces of plastic wrap. Using a wooden meat mallet or the side of a cleaver, pound vigorously until each slice is very thin and about 10 inches across. Mix flour with salt and ground black pepper.

SANDWICH:

Pork loin slices (see left)

4 large sandwich buns, lightly toasted if desired

Mustard

Mayonnaise

Dill pickle chips

Ketchup

Sliced onion

Lettuce

Vegetable oil for frying

Water

1/2 cup yellow cornmeal

Heat 1/2-inch of oil in a deep, 12-inch-wide skillet to 365 degrees. Dip each slice of pork in water, then in flour mixture. Pat both sides with cornmeal. Fry tenderloins, one at a time, turning once, until golden brown on both sides, about 5 minutes total. Drain on paper towels and keep warm until all are cooked.

Serve prepared pork on buns with desired condiments.

Yield: 4 sandwiches

In the pork-producing states of Indiana, Iowa, and Illinois, the traditional sandwich of choice is known as "the tenderloin" or, in some areas, "the breaded tenderloin." The sandwich is made from king-size boneless pork tenderloin that has been pounded to about a quarter-inch thick, breaded, and then fried, deep-fried, or sometimes grilled. These bun-busting monstrosities are generally served on toasted hamburger buns or Kaiser rolls, and condiments of choice consist of mustard, pickle, and onion. New initiates are sometimes alarmed by the sight of the tenderloin, which hangs out from the bun by at least an inch, and often much more, all the way around, creating a two-fisted dining experience.

According to road-food experts Jane and Michael Stern, Nicholas Freinstein of Huntington, Indiana, created the pork tenderloin sandwich. Freinstein peddled sandwiches from a basket before building a street cart that included a small grill, enabling him to cook tenderloins and burgers. Eventually, in 1908, Freinstein opened Nick's Kitchen in downtown Huntington. According to legend, his brother Jake, having suffered severe frostbite and the loss of his fingers, used his stumps to tenderize the slices of pork loin. Nick's competitors quickly adapted the tendering process by using wooden hammers or mechanical tenderizing devices, thereafter making it an integral part of the preparation of the tenderloin sandwich.

Diving Tower, Riverside Bathing Beach, Indianapolis, Ind.

Today, Nick's Kitchen is operated by Jean Anne Bailey, whose father purchased the business in 1969. Bailey prides herself on hefty tenderloins that are listed on her menu along with the challenge, "Bet You Need Both Hands." At Nick's, the tenderloins are first soaked in buttermilk and then dredged in coarsely ground cracker crumbs before frying. They're so popular that Bailey recently opened Nick's Sweet Shop in Wabash, where she offers her signature sandwich in addition to old-fashioned soda fountain favorites.

WHERE TO GO:

Nick's Kitchen
506 North Jefferson Street
Huntington, IN 46750
(260) 356-6618

Nick's Sweet Shop
35 West Market Street
Wabash, IN 46992
(260) 563-1312

The quintessential Midwest favorite called the loosemeat sandwich is hardly known outside the region unless one recalls an episode of the TV show "Roseanne," when it was featured as the Lunch Box Special of the house. Loosemeat sandwiches are, simply, twice-ground beef cooked and seasoned with a secret ingredient or two (depending upon the restaurant), piled into hamburger buns, and topped off with mustard, pickles, and/or chopped onions. Sometimes ketchup is available, but it's generally frowned upon.

Food sleuths Jane and Michael Stern uncovered the claim that David Heglin created the sandwich in 1924. He called it the Tavern and served it at his restaurant, Ye Old Tavern, in Sioux City, Iowa. However, the Maid-Rite restaurants have a counterclaim. They say Floyd Angell of Muscatine, Iowa, created it in 1926. Angell developed a special grind of meat, added some spices, cooked the meat loosely rather than forming it into a hamburger patty, placed it on a roll, and the result was a new ground beef sandwich. Legend has it that when Angell handed one of the sandwiches to a deliveryman, he remarked that the sandwich was "made right." Angell went on to establish the Maid-Rite restaurant chain in 1927, a franchise operation that today boasts more than eighty outlets in Iowa and other Midwestern states. An old rumor has it that Maid-Rite soaks the ground beef in beer and pickle juice, imparting a distinctive flavor, but the story has never been confirmed.

At Taylor's Maid-Rite in Marshalltown, Iowa, they butcher their own meat, which is then cooked in a 75-year-old "cooker" right up where all the customers can see what's going on and get a tantalizing whiff of the delicious aromas. Piled into buns, Maid-Rite loosemeat sandwiches are served with mustard, pickle, and onion (no ketchup is permitted). The sandwiches always come wrapped, even if they are eaten in-house, and they're always served with a spoon so that diners can scoop up every savory bite.

They keep things humming in —

Coon Rapids, Iowa

Come see the wheels go 'round.

WHERE TO GO:

The loosemeat sandwich is the flagship product of the Maid-Rite restaurant chain in Iowa and other Midwestern states. It's also featured at several independent restaurants.

Taylor's Maid-Rite
106 South Third Avenue
Marshalltown, IA 50158
(641) 753-9684

IOWA-STYLE LOOSEMEAT SANDWICHES

Commercial loosemeat sandwich formulas are closely guarded secrets.
This recipe, an amalgam of many suggestions, produces a terrific homemade version.

LOOSEMEAT:

1 pound twice-ground beef

1 tablespoon dried onion flakes

1 teaspoon ground black pepper

1/2 teaspoon salt

1 teaspoon sugar

2 teaspoons prepared yellow mustard

1 (12-ounce) can or bottle of beer (do not use light beer)

IN A MEDIUM FRYING PAN, brown the beef over medium-high heat, then drain it in a colander. Return beef to the pan and stir in the onion flakes, pepper, salt, sugar, mustard, and beer. Simmer, partially covered, over medium heat until liquid is evaporated, about 30 minutes.

SANDWICH:

Loosemeat (see left)

4 hamburger buns, toasted if desired

Fresh onion, chopped

Prepared yellow mustard

Pickles

SPOON BEEF INTO BUNS and serve immediately with condiments. Be sure to give everyone a spoon so they can scoop up any stray beef that escapes!

Yield: 4 sandwiches

NEED A QUICK FIX?

Taylor's Maid-Rite ships plain, frozen Maid-Rites door-to-door. Pickles and onions come too, in separate containers. You can order by phone (see left page) or via their web site at www.maidrite.com

Many early nineteenth-century Germans were attracted to the United States by the work of Gottfried Duden, a German businessman who wrote a series of letters home describing the new land in such glowing terms that they were ultimately published in a volume titled **A Report on a Journey to the Western States of North America.** Among other specifics in his report, Duden noted that there was ample opportunity for beer brewers, and it wasn't long before breweries sprang up across the country. This included places like Kansas, a state crisscrossed by numerous trails of commerce, with a need to cater to the thirsts of traders, soldiers, emigrants, and fortune seekers. By 1860, the brewing industry was Kansas' fourth largest industry, and by 1880, it boasted some ninety beer-brewing plants. In 1881, however, Kansas became the first state to enact Prohibition, heralding an end to breweries for the next 106 years. Also headed for an early demise, of course, were establishments like the Star of the West, a famous saloon in Leavenworth.

Lawrence, Kansas, was established in 1854, and the town quickly became recognized as a center of support for establishing Kansas as a "free state" in which slavery would not be tolerated. Its citizens fended off more than one attack by pro-slavery forces, standing tall as a symbol for the rights and freedoms of all individuals. That heritage was to manifest itself again in 1989 when, following Kansas' liberalization of liquor laws in 1987, The Free State Brewing Company opened for business. It was the state's first licensed brewery since 1881, and to many it has become a reincarnation of the old Star of the West saloon.

Owned by Chuck Magerl and located in the heart of Lawrence's renovated downtown historic district, The Free State Brewing Company is beloved by visitors and locals alike for its quality beers produced in the on-site brew house. Weekly selections may include such libations as John Brown Ale, Wheat State Golden, Ironman Imperial Stout, and Old Bachus Barleywine. The premises itself was at one time a trolley station, and interested groups can arrange tours of the brew house under the expert guidance of a master brewer.

REINISCH MEMORIAL ROSE GARDEN, GAGE PARK, TOPEKA, KANSAS—7

By law, brewpubs in Kansas must also serve food, and in the case of The Free State Brewing Company, that mandate provides an added bonus to patrons. Chef Rick Martin's menu offers the perfect balance of old favorites and his innovative, palate-teasing selections that include at least one daily vegetarian special. An all-time favorite on the menu is the Portobello Parmesan Sandwich, a delicious creation that's hefty enough to win the hearts of big, brawny, beer-loving guys.

PORTOBELLO PARMESAN SANDWICH

Reprinted with permission from Chuck Magerl, proprietor,
The Free State Brewing Company, Lawrence, Kansas

SUN-DRIED TOMATO PESTO:

1/2 cup sun-dried tomatoes

4 large cloves garlic

3 sprigs fresh or 1 teaspoon dried oregano

1/2 cup freshly grated Parmesan cheese

1/3 cup pine nuts (pignola nuts)

1/2 teaspoon kosher salt

1/2 cup extra virgin olive oil

PLACE ALL INGREDIENTS except olive oil in a food processor and pulse until mixture consists of fine pieces; with the machine running, gradually add the olive oil and process to a paste. Place pesto in a covered container and refrigerate until ready to use.

Yield: approximately 1 cup

WHERE TO GO:

The Free State Brewing Company
636 Massachusetts Street
Lawrence, KS 66044
(785) 843-4555
www.freestatebrewing.com

MUSHROOMS:

4 large Portobello mushrooms

1/2 cup olive oil

Salt and freshly ground black pepper to taste

1/4 cup flour for dredging

2 eggs, lightly beaten

1/4 cup milk

3/4 cup Panko (Japanese breadcrumbs)

1/4 cup freshly grated Parmesan cheese

1 quart canola or peanut oil for frying

PREHEAT THE OVEN to 400 degrees. Carefully de-stem the mushrooms using a very sharp knife, if necessary, to remove any woody part of the stem. With a grapefruit spoon or soup spoon, carefully scrape the underside gills from the cap and discard them. Bottom side up, generously brush the caps with olive oil, then repeat on the top side, using about 2 tablespoons olive oil per mushroom. Place the mushrooms on a cookie sheet with raised edges and season them with salt and pepper to taste. Bake the mushrooms for 10 minutes, or until slightly soft. Remove from oven and cool.

Place flour in a wide, flat dish or pie plate or on a piece of waxed paper. Whisk together the eggs and milk to make an egg wash and place in another wide, flat dish or pie plate. Combine Panko and Parmesan cheese in a third wide, flat dish or pie plate.

Heat the canola or peanut oil in a deep 12-inch frying pan to 325 degrees. Dredge each mushroom in the flour, dip in the egg wash, and then coat with breadcrumb mix. Fry the mushrooms, 2 at a time, until browned, about 2 minutes per side, and drain on paper toweling in a warm place.

SANDWICH:

4 sandwich-size portions of freshly baked rosemary focaccia bread, sliced crosswise

Sun-dried tomato pesto (see page 47)

8 thin slices provolone cheese

Fried mushrooms (see left)

Pepperoncini for garnish (optional)

Mixed greens with roasted red pepper vinaigrette dressing (optional)

PREHEAT THE BROILER and lay the sliced focaccia on a baking sheet. Spread each top slice of bread with sun-dried tomato pesto to taste, then lay a slice of provolone cheese on each top and bottom slice. Place bread under the broiler and broil until cheese is melted and golden brown. Remove from broiler, place a fried mushroom on each bottom slice of bread, cover with the top, and slice the sandwiches diagonally. Serve immediately, garnished with pepperoncini and accompanied by a mixed green salad, if desired.

Yield: 4 sandwiches

WATER JUMP, FORT RILEY, KANSAS

The Hot Brown

Reprinted with permission from the Camberley Brown Hotel,
Louisville, Kentucky

SAUCE:

1/2 cup butter

1/2 cup flour

4 cups milk

6 tablespoons freshly grated Parmesan cheese

1 beaten egg, room temperature

1 ounce whipped cream (optional)

Salt and freshly ground black pepper to taste

IN A LARGE SAUCEPAN, melt butter over medium heat. Whisk in flour to make a thick roux. Whisking constantly, gradually add the milk; cook slowly, whisking frequently, for 5 to 10 minutes to remove any taste of raw flour. Whisk in the Parmesan cheese and let the mixture cool slightly. Add the egg to thicken the sauce, but do not allow the sauce to boil or it will curdle. Remove from heat, and fold in whipped cream if desired. Season the sauce with salt and pepper to taste. Set aside and keep warm.

WHERE TO GO:

Camberley Brown Hotel
Thoroughbred Lounge
335 West Broadway
Louisville, KY 40202
(502) 583-0302
www.brownhotel.com

SANDWICH:

12 slices white bread, toasted

2 ½ to 3 pounds thinly sliced roast turkey

Sauce (see left)

Freshly grated Parmesan cheese for topping

12 strips bacon, cooked crisp and drained

PREHEAT BROILER. For each Hot Brown, place two slices of toast on a metal or flameproof dish. Cover the toast with a liberal amount of turkey. Pour a generous amount of sauce over the turkey and the toast. Sprinkle with additional grated Parmesan cheese. Place the entire dish under the broiler until the sauce is speckled brown and bubbly. Remove from broiler, cross two pieces of bacon over the top, and serve immediately.

Yield: 6 sandwiches

NOTE: Cissy Gregg, food editor for *The Courier-Journal* in Louisville from 1942 until the early 1960s, recommended using ½ cup grated cheddar and ½ cup grated Parmesan for the preparation of what she called the Louisville Hot Brown.

A chef named Fred K. Schmidt, who worked at Louisville's Brown Hotel, devised the legendary Hot Brown sandwich so favored by Kentuckians. When it first opened in 1923, the hotel's nightly dinner dances drew more than 1,200 guests. At the end of the evening, people in search of something to eat would head for the dining room. It wasn't long before they tired of the usual ham and eggs, and when Chef Schmidt produced The Hot Brown, an open-face turkey sandwich bathed in a delicate cheese sauce, society was delighted and a tradition was born. The sandwich became so popular that it spread throughout Kentucky and even beyond state borders. Back at the Brown Hotel, it was also featured on the regular menu where it became a favorite of the "ladies who lunch" crowd.

Although The Hot Brown is listed on many a restaurant menu in the upper South, perhaps the best place to sample it is at the Camberley Brown Hotel in Louisville. Built in 1923 by local philanthropist J. Graham Brown, the hotel has served as a major center for Louisville social life since its opening. Today, The Thoroughbred in The Camberley Brown Hotel lists the sandwich on its menu as "The Hot Brown."

While there are lots of different recipes for The Hot Brown, they always include a rich cheese sauce, often made with Parmesan, cheddar, or Swiss. The sandwich is commonly composed of one or two slices of toasted white bread topped with thin slices of turkey or chicken, country ham or crisp bacon, and sliced tomato. Covered with cheese sauce and sprinkled with Parmesan cheese, the sandwich is quickly browned under the broiler.

While most people think of the Creole and Cajun influence on the food of New Orleans, the Italians, too, have made a deep impact upon the cooking of southern Louisiana. Italian immigrants, especially those from Sicily, arrived in significant numbers during the 1880s and 1890s. Many had been employed in the citrus trade in Italy, and they found work on Louisiana's plantations. Others settled in the French Quarter and became involved in the food industry, opening grocery stores, bakeries, and food-processing plants.

It is said that Italian workers employed at the markets in New Orleans would commonly scoop broken olives from barrels and add them to the round loves of bread they brought for lunch. The loaves were called "muffs," and sandwiches with the addition of olives were eventually called muffalettas. One of those early immigrants was Signor Lupo Salvadore, who, in 1906, established the now-famous Central Grocery in New Orleans' French Quarter. Salvadore is credited with the creation of the muffaletta that we know today. He apparently took note of what the workers were eating, embellished it a bit, and sold made-to-order sandwiches from his grocery.

Bartolomeo Perrone, who came from Palermo, Sicily, established Progress Grocery, a long-time competitor of Central Grocery, in 1924. (Progress Grocery was sold in 2001, and the business now operates under the name of Luigi's Fine Foods.) Progress, too, claimed to have invented the muffaletta. It was, as the story goes, a relative of the old Progress Grocery family who first baked muffaletta bread in New Orleans sometime around 1895. (Of interest is the fact that muffaletta bread is still made in at least one old-fashioned neighborhood bakery in Piano degli Albanese, near Palermo, Sicily, home of an Albanian colony since the fifteenth century.) One might thus speculate that the families of both Progress Grocery and Central Grocery had a direct hand in the creation of the muffaletta sandwich, which boasts a combination of Italian and Albanian heritage.

Today, the muffaletta is on the menus of numerous New Orleans restaurants and is one of the city's signature sandwiches. (The po-boy, in many different variations, is another.) Virtually no tourist visits the Big Easy without trying a muffaletta, and many folks grab a few extras to enjoy on the plane trip home.

The key to a great muffaletta sandwich is in the bread, the use of fresh, premium cold cuts, and the olive salad that's included as a garnish. The bread is prepared in ten- or twelve-inch rounds and topped with sesame seeds. Since it seems to be made only in New Orleans, a common substitute is a round of crusty Italian bread.

Called "the Holy Grail of sandwich fillings" by Chuck Taggart, author of the popular Internet site www.gumbopages.com, olive salad is absolutely crucial to the muffaletta. Without it, you won't have the real thing. Some versions, like that sold at Luigi's Fine Foods, contain cauliflower and carrots in addition to the traditional ingredients.

The bread is sliced in half and layered with very fresh, high-quality cold cuts: thinly sliced mortadella (Italian salami), ham, Genoa salami, mozzarella cheese, and provolone cheese. A healthy addition of olive salad crowns the filling that is then capped with the top of the loaf. The sandwich, because of its size, is typically cut into quarters for serving.

THE MUFFALETTA

OLIVE SALAD:

1 (10-ounce) jar pimiento-stuffed green olives, drained and chopped

3 cloves garlic, minced

2 tablespoons drained marinated cocktail onions

2 large celery stalks, halved lengthwise and thinly sliced

1 tablespoon drained capers

1 $1/2$ teaspoons dried oregano

$1/2$ teaspoon ground black pepper

1 $1/2$ tablespoons red wine vinegar

3 tablespoons olive oil

COMBINE ALL INGREDIENTS in a medium bowl and stir well. Cover and refrigerate for at least 4 hours to allow flavors to blend. Bring to room temperature before using. Mixture may be stored for up to 2 weeks if kept in a tightly covered container and refrigerated.

Yield: about 2 cups

OREGANO ONIONS (GARNISH):

2 medium onions, thinly sliced

1 teaspoon dried oregano

$1/4$ cup extra virgin olive oil

$1/2$ cup apple cider vinegar

SEPARATE ONION RINGS and place in a medium bowl. Add remaining ingredients and mix well. Cover and let stand at room temperature for 1 to 2 hours. For longer storage, cover tightly and refrigerate. Bring to room temperature before using. Oregano onions are an excellent garnish for muffalettas and po-boys.

Yield: about 1 $1/2$ cups

NOTE: The recipe for Oregano Onions is reprinted with permission from *Too Good To Be True* by the late Chet Beckwith of Baton Rouge, Louisiana—a fantastic cook and dear friend who is sorely missed.

SANDWICH:

1 (10- to 12-inch) round muffaletta bread or crusty Italian bread

1/4 pound thinly sliced mozzarella cheese

1/4 pound thinly sliced provolone cheese

1/2 pound thinly sliced Genoa or hard salami

1/2 pound thinly sliced mortadella sausage

1/2 pound thinly sliced capicolla (optional)

1/2 pound thinly sliced baked ham

1 to 2 cups olive salad, to taste (see page 53)

1 cup oregano onions (see page 53), to taste (optional)

Extra virgin olive oil (optional)

BRING ALL INGREDIENTS to room temperature before assembling the sandwich. Preheat oven to 350 degrees. Slice the loaf of muffaletta or Italian bread in half horizontally, place on a baking sheet, and heat in oven for 5 minutes, or until lightly toasted.

Remove bread from oven. Evenly distribute slices of mozzarella cheese on the top half and evenly distribute slices of provolone cheese on the bottom half. Return bread to oven and bake for 5 to 7 minutes, or until cheese is softened but not melted. Remove from oven. On the bottom half, layer the meats, beginning with the Genoa or hard salami, then the mortadella, the capicolla (optional), and finally, the ham. Press down lightly on the meats to create a level surface and spoon on the olive salad. Add oregano onions and drizzle with olive oil if desired. Cover with top half of bread, slice into quarters, and serve immediately.

Yield: 4 sandwiches

NOTE: Capicolla and oregano onions are a nontraditional but delicious addition to the muffaletta sandwich.

NEED A QUICK FIX?

No time to make your own muffalettas? Don't despair. The world famous sandwich can be shipped to you straight from New Orleans. Take your pick of Central Grocery or Progress Grocery. Although the latter no longer exists, having been bought by new owners who operate under the name of Luigi's Fine Foods, the Perrone family sells its products by mail order under the name of Progress Grocery. Both firms sell muffalettas as well as olive salad. Muffaletta bread and a full range of Italian cold cuts are available from Progress.

Central Grocery
923 Decatur Street
New Orleans, LA 70116
(504) 523-1620

Progress Grocery
(504) 455-FOOD [3663]
(866) 455-3663 toll free
(504) 455-3660 fax
www.progressgrocery.com

WHERE TO GO:

Central Grocery
923 Decatur Street
New Orleans, LA 70116
(504) 523-1620

Luigi's Fine Foods
(formerly Progress Grocery)
915 Decatur Street
New Orleans, LA 70116
(504) 529-4975

MAINE

Oh sturdy Maine, so true and brave.
Thou launchest fleets upon the wave.
Virtue and courage are thine own,
Thy chosen emblem
a Pine Cone.

PINE CONE
MAINE STATE CARD

STATE CAPITOL, AUGUSTA MAINE   6223

There is as much controversy over who developed the original lobster roll as there is discussion over the proper preparation of this pedigreed New England sandwich. Certainly, it is a luxurious and tasty treat containing plenty of fresh cooked lobster. Once prevalent, and yet disdained by early colonists, who fed it to their pigs, lobster today commands premium prices.

Very little information is available as to the actual debut of the lobster roll. John Mariani says in **The Encyclopedia of American Food & Drink** that Harry Perry, owner of Perry's in Milford, Connecticut, may have devised it in the 1920s. He adds that Perry supposedly had a sign hanging up from 1927 until 1977 proclaiming his establishment as the "Home of the Famous Lobster Roll." Jean Anderson confirms that the lobster roll is clearly a twentieth-century invention, and her version in **The American Century Cookbook** is based on the hamburger roll, which wasn't manufactured until 1912.

An investigation conducted by the Maine Lobster Promotion Council unearthed a counterclaim. According to Bill Bayley of Bayley's Lobster Pound in Scarborough, Maine, his grandmother began selling leftover lobster from her kitchen window in 1915. By the early 1930s, Mrs. Bayley sold lobster salad and shortly thereafter began selling lobster sandwiches on regular crustless bread. Somewhere along the line, bread was substituted with hot dog rolls, creating the lobster roll that's still sold at Bayley's today.

The popularity of the lobster roll is evident throughout coastal New England, where it can be found in establishments ranging from posh restaurants to take-out seafood shacks. Lobster rolls also take center stage at luncheons and suppers held by churches and nonprofit organizations, especially in Connecticut and Maine.

Tourists familiar with Maine's famous lobsters equate lobster rolls with the perfect casual seaside meal along the state's coastline. Many flock to the state in August when Lobster Month is celebrated. Red's Eats in Wiscasset, Maine, has been in business since 1938 and serves a lobster roll par excellence—a whole lobster, with both claw and tail meat, is served up in a buttered and toasted bun. Owner Allen "Red" Gagnon has neatly resolved the butter-versus-mayonnaise controversy by serving both on the side, and everyone seems to be happy. In 1999, **Yankee Magazine** picked Red's Eats as one of the most outstanding reasons to visit Maine. Housed in a 20-x-18-foot building, Red's is strictly take-out but provides a few picnic tables where visitors can sit and enjoy those luxurious lobster rolls.

There are two very distinct camps of opinion surrounding the correct preparation of a lobster roll. In its purest form, chunks of fresh, hot lobster are gently laid into a buttered hot dog roll, melted butter is poured lavishly over all, and the sandwich is served immediately. Contenders opt for lobster dressed with mayonnaise, celery, and perhaps some kind of seasoning, such as lemon juice and grated onion, spooned into a warm hot dog bun. The latter is often topped with shredded lettuce, an act that many classify as nothing short of heresy. Most everyone agrees that the proper bun to use for a lobster roll is a hot dog bun that's cut on the top, rather than the sides, as it makes for easier loading.

LUSCIOUS LOBSTER ROLLS

Perhaps the best way to savor pricey lobster is to avoid frills and keep it simple.
Seafood shacks along the New England coast do a land-office business
catering to a public that adheres to this culinary rule.

2 large lobster tails

1 cup warm melted butter

4 quality hot dog or sausage rolls,
   top-cut if possible

WHERE TO GO:

Red's Eats
Water and Main Streets
Wiscasset, ME 04578
(207) 882-6128

NEED A QUICK FIX?

Maine lobster can be ordered from:

Bayley's Lobster Pound
Pine Point
Jones Creek Drive and Avenue 6
P.O. Box 304
Scarborough, ME 04074
(207) 883-4571
(800) WE-BOIL-M [932-6456] toll free

PREHEAT GRILL and brush lightly with oil to keep lobster from sticking to grate. Remove lobster from shells, keeping the tails intact. Grill lobster tails over medium-high heat, brushing with melted butter, just until cooked through. Remove from grill and keep warm.

Preheat broiler and lightly toast the rolls. Cut each lobster tail in half lengthwise or chop the tail into half-inch pieces. Place a half tail or equivalent in each toasted bun and serve with remaining melted butter to drizzle over the lobster.

Yield: 4 sandwiches

NOTE: Whole lobsters weighing about 1 pound may be used. Plunge them into rapidly boiling water and cook 7 to 10 minutes. Drain, extract meat, and chop it into $1/2$-inch pieces.

HILL'S SOUTHERN MARYLAND STUFFED HAM

Reprinted with permission from Kevin Hill, proprietor,
St. Mary's Landing, Charlotte Hall, Maryland

STUFFING:

4 pounds fresh kale

4 pounds fresh cabbage

1 bunch celery (stalks only)

1 medium onion

1 pound watercress (optional)

$1/4$ cup mustard seed

$1/4$ cup celery seed

$1/4$ cup crushed red pepper

$1/4$ cup salt

$1/4$ cup ground white pepper

3 tablespoons ground red pepper

COARSELY CHOP KALE, cabbage, celery, onion, and watercress into $1/2$- to 1-inch pieces and place in a very large bowl. In a medium bowl, combine the spices; mix the spices into the stuffing.

HAM:

Stuffing (see left)

1 (16- to 18-pound) de-boned corned ham

GENEROUSLY STUFF THE BONE CAVITY of the ham. Make about 6 very deep slits in other sections of the ham and push additional stuffing into them. Tie the ends and midsection of the ham with butcher's twine and place any leftover stuffing on top of the ham. Wrap the ham in cheesecloth or use a new white pillowcase, tightly securing the wrapping.

Place a wire rack in the bottom of a very large pot (to keep the ham from burning), fill with 6 to 8 quarts of water, and bring the water to a rolling boil. Carefully place the ham into the water and simmer it for 15 minutes per pound. It is important not to overcook the ham.

It's also important to cool the ham quickly in order to avoid any possible contamination. Cooling can be accomplished in two ways: (1) remove the ham from the pot and place it directly into enough ice and water to completely cover it; add ice frequently until the ham is cooled, about 2 hours; or (2) remove the ham from the pot and let it cool for 5 minutes; with a large knife, cut the ham into quarters and tightly wrap each quarter in film or aluminum foil; place in the freezer for a half hour, then store it in the refrigerator or unwrap the ham and slice it for serving.

SANDWICH:

2 slices white, wheat, or rye bread

Mustard or mayonnaise

Southern Maryland stuffed ham (see left), sliced, enough for 1 sandwich

SPREAD SLICES of bread with mustard or mayonnaise; layer ham on one slice, top with remaining slice, cut in half diagonally, and serve.

Yield: 1 sandwich

A little-known delicacy of southern Maryland is the stuffed ham, the making of which is a laborious effort that eventually delivers one of the finest sandwiches in America. Typically, an eighteen-pound Maryland corned ham is boned, then stuffed with ten or twelve pounds of kale, cabbage, watercress, celery, and onion spiced with mustard seed and various peppers. The ham is simmered, then cooled and sliced. Served on a choice of bread, Maryland stuffed ham produces a sandwich so good that it has withstood the test of time for more than 200 years.

Hogs were, of course, a mainstay of the colonial diet, and the annual butchering always took place in the fall. On southern Maryland's flourishing tobacco plantations, the slaves were given the less-desirable cuts of the hog, including the head. Using what was at hand, they stuffed the hog's head with fall vegetables, seasoned it with peppers, and slowly simmered their humble meal until tender. So delectable was the result that it wasn't long before the plantation owners adopted the preparation for their hams.

The availability of stuffed ham is generally seasonal; it makes its appearance mainly at Thanksgiving, Christmas, and Easter, when it's sold by the ham or by the slice at just about any grocery store in St. Mary's County. Many families still prepare their own hams from recipes that have been kept secret for generations. Since the ham is normally served cold, it makes the perfect filling for sandwiches. Pilgrims to southern Maryland in search of tasty stuffed ham are well advised to head for St. Mary's Landing, where owner Kevin Hill carries on a family tradition of serving it year-round. Maryland stuffed-ham sandwiches are available any time of day, and patrons happily place their orders for sandwiches, with mustard or mayonnaise, on white, wheat, or rye bread. For breakfast, St. Mary's Landing serves the ham on traditional Southern biscuits.

WHERE TO GO:

St. Mary's Landing
29935 Three Notch Road
Charlotte Hall, MD 20622
(301) 884-6124

Mattingly's Finer Foods (seasonal: stuffed hams and stuffed ham sandwiches)
Leonardtown, MD 20650
(301) 475-9201

A relative newcomer to the American sandwich scene is the "Vietnamese sub," or bánh mi, which reflects the influence that one of America's most recent immigrant groups has exerted on our sandwich culture.

The bánh mi is based on mini French baguettes (baguettine), an inheritance from the French colonial period in Vietnam. According to a post on the Internet's Chowhound site, bread isn't native to Vietnam, where it's considered food for the poor who cannot afford rice. Food writer Kate Heyhoe notes that the bánh mi baguette is made with both wheat and rice flour, resulting in a much lighter loaf and a crispier crust. During French colonial days, sandwiches made from these baguettes were sold in expensive food shops catering to the French colonists and to "French wannabes," for whom it became a status symbol in the 1940s and 1950s. These sandwiches almost always included mayonnaise, raw green onion, and whatever an individual might order for the filling.

It wasn't long before imitations of the sandwich, called báhn mi tay, made their appearance in stores catering to the Vietnamese. The xe bánh mi (literally translated as "vehicle selling bread"), sold from boxes mounted on tricycles, soon followed. This last version was cheaper and essentially more Vietnamese because it primarily featured inexpensive ingredients like cucumber, green pepper, pickled vegetables, and herbs much loved by the Vietnamese people.

By the 1960s, the original French sandwiches eaten by the colonials had pretty much disappeared from Vietnam along with the French themselves. Following the Vietnam War and reunification of Vietnam under the Communists, thousand of Vietnamese fled their homeland, many coming to the United States. These immigrants brought with them the bánh mi, and it soon made its appearance in Vietnamese sandwich shops that they established throughout the country.

The bánh mi is an explosion of flavors and contrasts that has caught the fancy of the American sandwich-eating public. Some aficionados, unclear as to the actual content of the sandwich, simply describe it as "filled with strange and wonderful things."

Fresh baguettes are typically toasted or heated, then filled with ingredients such as pickled daikon, carrot, and hot peppers, along with onion, cucumber, and cilantro. A choice of meat, ranging from barbecued pork, cured ham, chicken, or Vietnamese bologna, is accompanied by pâté (usually pork or chicken liver). Finally, a dressing of Vietnamese hot chili sauce or soy sauce and vinegar delivers additional punch to this tasty and exotic sandwich. It should be noted that some Vietnamese sandwich shops in the United States do serve bánh mi with mayonnaise that is spicy-sweet or that has a vinegary bite to it.

Saigon Sandwich Shop, a Vietnamese take-out shop located on Boston's revitalized Washington Street, is a local favorite that specializes in a curried chicken version of the bánh mi as well as delicious meat-filled spring rolls. Two other sources favored by local fans of the bánh mi are on Beach Street. Thai Binh Market has a bánh mi counter in the front, where the hands-down favorite is the hot beef. Across the street is Mix Bakery, featuring a sizable roster of bánh mi, including chicken, cold cuts, and tofu.

In his food letter **Simple Cooking,** John Thorne, one of America's most celebrated food writers, presents a wonderful essay entitled "Bánh Mi and Me," in which he describes both his discovery of this exotic sandwich and his subsequent mission to uncover how it is made. We thank John for sharing with us the fruits of his labor.

BÁNH MI

Reprinted with permission from Simple Cooking, the food letter written
and published by John and Matt Thorne at www.outlawcook.com

THE BREAD:

This can be an entire French (or Italian) light crusty roll or a wedge cut from a bâtarde (the next bread size up from a baguette). If it's not fresh from the bakery, heat it for 5 minutes in a warm oven before making the sandwich.

THE SPREAD:

Choose one or more of the following: mayonnaise, hot sauce, pork or chicken liver pâté, sweet butter, Maggi seasoning, a drizzle of Nuoc Cham (see page 62). I like pâté spread on one side and Nuoc Cham mixed into mayonnaise on the other.

THE TOPPING:

Consider these mandatory: thinly sliced European cucumber, marinated slivers of daikon and carrot (Cu Cai Carot Chua—see page 62) or carrot alone, and lots of fresh coriander. Optional extras include sliced jicama, a few basil or mint leaves, some slivers of scallion (or very thinly sliced onion), and slices of fiery hot chile pepper.

THE FILLING:

One or more different kinds of Vietnamese cold cuts (look in the freezer section of your Asian grocery), preferably from a pork loaf (white) and a cured ham (pink). A reasonable supermarket substitute would be a few slices of chicken loaf and boiled ham. Those leery of cold cuts in general might try thin slices of roast pork, grilled mushrooms, or slices of firm tofu, drained and then marinated in Nuoc Cham overnight.

NUOC CHAM (VIETNAMESE DIPPING SAUCE):

1 clove garlic

$1/2$ teaspoon ground chile paste

1 Thai chile pepper, seeded (optional, see Cook's Note)

2 tablespoons fish sauce (see Cook's Note)

1 tablespoon fresh lime juice with pulp

$1/3$ cup hot water

2 tablespoons sugar

PUT THE GARLIC, chile paste, and optional Thai pepper into a mortar or food processor and pulverize into a paste. Combine this mixture with the rest of the ingredients in a small bowl and stir until the sugar has dissolved. This sauce can be kept in the refrigerator for 1 month.

Yield: $3/4$ cup

COOK'S NOTE: Thai chile peppers are small and intensely hot. Any small fiery (or not so fiery!) chile pepper can be substituted. Fish sauce, or nuoc mam, is an essential element of Vietnamese cuisine. It is made by packing anchovies in salt and drawing off the brine; the best brands contain no other ingredients. Apply with a light hand.

CU CAI CAROT CHUA (CARROT AND DAIKON IN VINEGAR):

1 medium carrot

1 small daikon (sweet white radish)

1 cup water

2 teaspoons rice vinegar

2 teaspoons sugar

1 pinch salt

PEEL THE CARROT and radish and cut each into 2-inch lengths. Either grate coarsely into long strands or, with a sharp knife or vegetable peeler, cut each length into paper-thin strips. Put the rest of the ingredients in a small bowl and stir until the sugar completely dissolves. Marinate the strips of carrot and radish in this mixture for at least 1 hour or as long as overnight. Remove the vegetables from the liquid before using. If marinated carrots alone are preferred, omit the daikon and cut the marinade proportions in half.

WHERE TO GO:

The following locations are all in Boston's Chinatown:

Saigon Sandwich Company, Inc.
696 Washington Street
Boston, MA 02116
(617) 542-6296

Thai Binh Market (Pacific Supermarket)
15 Beach Street
Boston, MA 02111
(617) 426-2771

Mix Bakery
Beach Street (across from Thai Binh Market)
Boston, MA 02111

MICHIGAN PASTIES

The recipe for pasty dough is reprinted with permission from Geraldine Duncann, food writer and culinary anthropologist, while the filling for these pasties is adapted from several traditional Michigan pasty recipes.

DOUGH:

5 cups all-purpose flour

1 pound cold butter

1 egg

1 tablespoon vinegar

Water

PLACE FLOUR in a large mixing bowl and add butter, cut into tablespoon-size chunks. With a wire pastry blender, work the butter into the flour until the mixture reaches the consistency of coarse cornmeal.

.

Put 1 egg and the tablespoon of vinegar in a 1-cup measure and fill to 1 cup with cold water. Add to the flour mixture and, using a table fork, stir the mixture round and round until the mixture gathers into a ball. Turn the mixture out onto a lightly floured board and knead it very gently. The goal is not to knead it but, rather, push it together into a cohesive ball of dough. Pat the dough into a flat disk, wrap it in plastic wrap, and chill thoroughly, about 2 to 3 hours, before rolling it out.

FILLING:

$1^1/4$ pounds coarsely ground beef (80 percent lean)

$1/2$ pound coarsely ground pork or spicy pork sausage

$1^1/2$ cups chopped onion

1 cup diced rutabaga or turnip

1 cup diced potato

1 teaspoon pepper

1 teaspoon salt

$1/4$ cup chopped fresh parsley or 2 tablespoons dried parsley

IN A LARGE BOWL, combine all ingredients for the filling. Using your hands, mix together until the vegetables are thoroughly incorporated into the meat.

In Michigan's Upper Peninsula, the pasty (pass-tee) reigns as the portable, hand-held meal of choice. It's what one might call a hand-held pie version of the sandwich, consisting of dough that encases tasty fillings of meat and vegetables, baked and served hot. Some folks like their pasties served with gravy, and new versions include vegetarian offerings as well as the breakfast pasty filled with ham, bacon, eggs, onions, cheese, and potatoes.

Although it is not known when the pasty originated, it's attributed to Cornwall, England, where citations have been found in literature dating to the twelfth century. In later years, Cornwall's underground tin miners typically carried hot pasties in their pockets to be eaten for lunch. In the early 1800s, miners from Cornwall immigrated to Michigan's Upper Peninsula to find work in the copper mines, and they brought with them their pasty tradition. In the mines, pasties were warmed on a shovel held over headlamp candles. Their popularity spread among the many ethnic groups who settled the region, and today, pasties are a favorite dish of folks known as Yoopers in the Upper Peninsula, making their appearance at numerous celebrations and fundraising events.

Restaurants throughout the Upper Peninsula feature pasties on their menus. A favorite source for pasties are those made by the residents and kitchen staff of the Still Waters Assisted Living Community in Calumet, Michigan. The residents, many of whom are octogenarians, so enjoy their pasties that they began making their own. It wasn't long before they began selling a few to locals; word spread, and the operation took off. Today, the pasties are sold to regional restaurants, locals, and visitors, as well as throughout the country via an Internet site called Pasty Central. Proceeds from the nonprofit operation go to Still Waters' reserve fund.

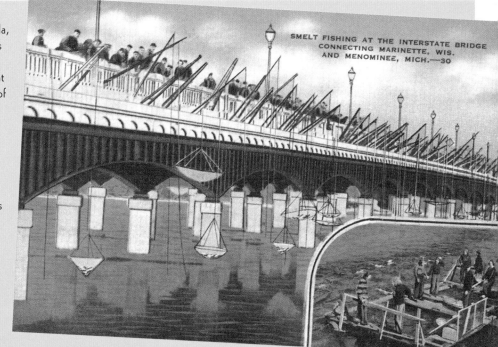

SMELT FISHING AT THE INTERSTATE BRIDGE CONNECTING MARINETTE, WIS. AND MENOMINEE, MICH.—30

NEED A QUICK FIX?

Pasty Central ships their product throughout the country.

PASTY:

1 egg

1 tablespoon water

Cooking spray

Dough (see page 64)

Filling (see page 64)

PREHEAT THE OVEN to 400 degrees. In a small bowl, beat together the egg and water. Prepare three rimmed cookie sheets with a light coating of cooking spray.

Remove pasty dough from the refrigerator and divide it into 6 equal pieces. Roll out each piece of dough to a thickness of about $1/8$-inch and a diameter of 9 inches. Place 1 cup of the pasty filling on one half of each circle, and spread it out to within $1/2$ inch of the edges of the half. Carefully fold the other half of the dough over it, crimp the edges together well with a fork, and place pasties on baking sheets. With a sharp knife, cut a 1-inch slit in the top of each pasty; brush them well with the egg wash. Bake the pasties for 50 to 60 minutes, or until they are golden brown and crispy. Remove from oven and let pasties rest 5 minutes before serving.

Yield: 6 pasties

Where to Go:

Pasty Central/Still Waters
26096 East Elm Street
Calumet, MI 49913
(906) 337-5979
(877) PASTY-11 (727-8911) toll-free
www.pasty.com

The web site also lists several businesses throughout Michigan's Upper Peninsula that sell pasties made at Still Waters.

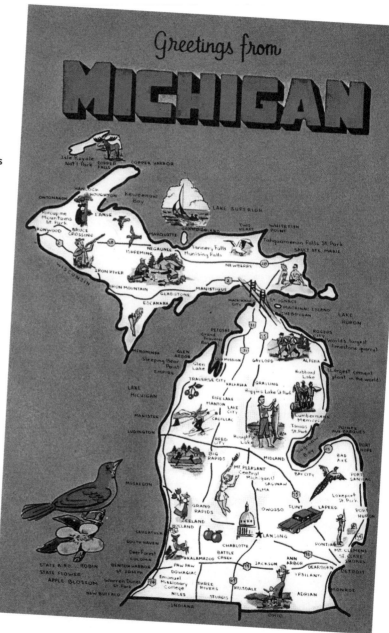

MINNESOTA FRIED WALLEYE SANDWICH

This delicious recipe is adapted from several traditional Minnesota recipes for fried walleye that always emphasize the use of cracker crumbs.

WALLEYE FILLETS:

1 1/2 pounds walleye fillets, about 1 inch thick

1 cup finely crushed saltine crackers

1/2 teaspoon salt, to taste

1 teaspoon ground black pepper, to taste

1/2 teaspoon garlic powder, to taste (optional—see Note)

1 egg, lightly beaten

1/4 cup milk

1 cup butter-flavored shortening (such as Crisco brand)

1/2 cup butter

RINSE THE WALLEYE FILLETS under cold running water and drain well on paper towels. If necessary, use a sharp knife to trim and cut the fillets into 4 equal pieces.

In a wide, shallow dish or pie plate, combine the cracker crumbs, salt, pepper, and garlic powder if using. In another wide, shallow dish or pie plate, combine the egg and milk, mixing well.

In a deep 12-inch frying pan, melt the butter-flavored shortening and butter over medium heat. Meanwhile, dip each piece of walleye in the egg mixture, letting the excess drip off, then lightly coat the fish with cracker crumbs. Fry the walleye over medium heat about 5 to 7 minutes per side, turning once, until golden brown on both sides.

SANDWICH:

Walleye fillets (see left)

4 kaiser or bulkie-style rolls, toasted if desired

Lemon wedges

Tartar sauce (see page 104)

PLACE ONE FILLET on the bottom half of each roll, top with other half of the roll, and serve immediately, accompanied by lemon wedges and tartar sauce.

Yield: 4 sandwiches

NOTE: Minnesotans favor a touch of garlic when frying walleye while others prefer not to interfere with the mild taste of the fish. If walleye is not available, haddock makes an excellent substitute.

WHERE TO GO:

Tavern on Grand
656 Grand Avenue
St. Paul, MN 55105
(651) 228-9030

The walleye, a member of the perch family, has been Minnesota's official state fish since 1965. It's found throughout the thousands of lakes and rivers in Minnesota, making it the state's most popular sport fish. Named for its silvery, smoky eyes, comparable to those of "walleyed" domestic animals, the walleye is prized for its mild, savory flavor and versatility of preparation.

Visitors to the St. Paul area are likely to seek out restaurants where they can enjoy Minnesota's signature fish for breakfast, lunch, or dinner—sometimes, all three. Tavern on Grand, located on St. Paul's legendary Grand Avenue, is a popular neighborhood tavern that serves up a true taste of Minnesota. Even Mikhail Gorbachev, president of the U.S.S.R., popped in for a taste of fresh walleye back in 1990 on a visit to the United States. The décor is strictly that of a North Woods lake cabin, providing a real sense of atmosphere. Over a thousand pounds of walleye are served weekly, and it's featured on the menu in grilled or deep-fried versions. The latter calls for a light cracker meal coating that doesn't overpower the delicacy of the fish itself. While some diners enjoy fillets served with various side dishes, others opt for the popular walleye sandwich, which consists of a breaded, deep-fried fillet on a bun with lettuce and tomato.

Public Baths, St. Paul, Minn.

AJAX DINER'S FRIED CATFISH PO-BOY

Reprinted with permission from Ajax Diner, Oxford, Mississippi

SEASONED FRY CORNMEAL:

1/2 cup yellow cornmeal

1/4 cup flour

3/4 teaspoon kosher salt

1 1/2 teaspoons lemon pepper

1 1/2 teaspoons onion powder

1 1/2 teaspoons garlic powder

1 1/4 teaspoons cayenne pepper

COMBINE ALL ingredients, mixing well.

Yield: enough for about 5 (5- to 7-ounce) catfish fillets

CHANNEL CATFISH

SANDWICH:

Vegetable oil for frying

1 (5- to 7-ounce) Mississippi farm-raised catfish fillet

Seasoned cornmeal (see left)

French bread, about 7 to 8 inches long, halved crosswise, buttered, and lightly toasted

Mayonnaise to taste

Hamburger dill slices

Green cabbage, shredded

WHERE TO GO:

Ajax Diner
118 Courthouse Square
Oxford, MS 38655
(662) 232-8880

IN A VERY DEEP FRYING PAN or pot, preheat enough vegetable oil to completely submerge the catfish, to 350 degrees. Dredge the catfish in the seasoned cornmeal and fry it in the oil for 8 minutes; the catfish will float when it's done. Remove from oil and place on paper towels or a brown paper bag to drain.

Meanwhile, spread the top slice of the toasted French bread with mayonnaise to taste. Add a layer of hamburger dill slices and sprinkle with shredded green cabbage. Place the catfish on the bottom slice, sandwich the two halves together, cut it in half, and serve immediately.

Additional toppings may be added to taste, such as cheddar cheese, bacon, celery-seed-laced coleslaw, Jalapeño tartar sauce, or Louisiana or Tabasco hot sauce.

Yield: 1 sandwich

NOTE: After slicing open the French bread, you may wish to remove some of the interior bread, creating a kind of boat in which plenty of the filling ingredients can be placed. Sliced fresh tomatoes are also excellent in this sandwich.

Mississippi is the global leader in production of farm-raised catfish. In 1965, J. B. Williams dug his first catfish pond in Humphreys County, and others quickly followed his lead. So successful was the fledgling industry that by 1976 the area was dubbed the "Catfish Capital of the World."

Oxford, Mississippi, northeast of Humphreys County, is a college town. It has also been home to famous writers who, over the years, seem to have flocked into the area like homing pigeons. William Faulker settled in Oxford in 1930; John Grisham, author of legal thrillers, bought a farm near Oxford in 1990; and it's the birthplace of "grit-lit" author Larry Brown. Oxford is also the home of John T. Edge, director of the Southern Foodways Alliance at the University of Mississippi's Center for the Study of Southern Culture in Oxford and a nationally acclaimed food writer and cultural commentator.

It turns out that a favorite Oxford dining emporium for writers just happens to be the Ajax Diner, located right on the Square, and renowned, among other down-home Southern specialties, for its catfish po' boy. Cornmeal-battered and fried, the catfish is pure Mississippi goodness served on French bread and dressed with shredded green cabbage, pickle, and mayonnaise. John T. Edge says if you ask nicely, they'll even top off that catfish with a heap of celery-seed-laced coleslaw that elevates the sandwich to a little bit of heaven. A favorite go-with is Barq's root beer, which originated in New Orleans.

The St. Paul sandwich is a curiosity of St. Louis, a city with a penchant for creating odd sandwiches like those made with brains or snoots and ears. While one might assume that a sandwich with the moniker of "St. Paul" would have originated in Minnesota, food authorities claim that it has nothing whatsoever to do with that area. Rather, it's a noted specialty of many of the Chinese restaurants in the St. Louis, Missouri, area.

The origin of today's St. Paul sandwich may be an enigma, but reports say that it was a popular offering in St. Louis as far back as the 1960s and perhaps earlier; one source cites 1943. Most folks, including St. Louis writer Thomas Crone, believe that Chinese restaurateurs who wanted to tempt the sandwich-loving American palate created it. This theory maintains that the sandwich is based on egg foo yung, an old Chinese recipe that has become thoroughly Americanized. Others believe that St. Paul was originally another term for the Denver sandwich and later adapted by Chinese restaurateurs.

Plain old commercial white bread provides the underpinnings for the St. Paul sandwich. Then comes an egg foo yung patty, typically composed of eggs, onion, and bamboo shoots, and enhanced with plenty of salt or MSG. Unlike egg foo yung, however, the combination is not scrambled but deep-fried. The bread is generously slathered with mayonnaise, and the egg foo yung patty is added along with pickle, tomato, and lettuce.

For those who want to take their St. Paul a step beyond the "plain" version, there are various additions available, like shrimp, beef, chicken, pork, and ham. A "special" generally calls for three additional ingredients chosen from a list of options. Wrapped in white butcher's paper and encased in a brown paper bag, the St. Paul is an inexpensive moveable feast in a land of sandwich take-out options. St. Louis has numerous restaurants specializing in the St. Paul, and one of the favorites is Kim Van Restaurant, operated by a Vietnamese couple, Island and Jennifer Nguyen, with the occasional help of their two young daughters.

Municipal Free Bridge, St. Louis, Mo.

WHERE TO GO:

Kim Van Restaurant
2649 Gravois Avenue
St. Louis, MO 63118
(314) 865-1321

THE ST. PAUL SANDWICH

EGG FOO YUNG PATTIES:

3 eggs

$1/2$ teaspoon salt or MSG

$1/2$ cup diced cooked chicken breast

$1/2$ cup diced cooked ham

$1/4$ cup finely chopped green bell pepper

$1/4$ cup finely chopped onion

$1/2$ cup finely chopped bamboo shoots

$1/2$ cup finely chopped water chestnuts

Oil for deep-frying

BEAT THE EGGS, and season with salt or MSG. Add meat and vegetables, and mix well. Set aside.

In a deep frying pan, add oil to $1/4$-inch in depth. Heat oil over medium-high heat. Using a ladle, carefully but quickly add $1/2$ cup of egg mixture to oil. Baste the top of the patty with hot oil so it browns, and then, with a slotted spoon, flip the patty over, being careful not to splatter the oil. When golden brown on both sides, remove patty, drain on paper towels, and keep warm while frying remaining patties.

SANDWICH:

8 slices plain white bread

Mayonnaise

Lettuce

Egg foo yung patties (see left)

4 thin slices tomato

Pickle slices (optional)

TO ASSEMBLE SANDWICHES, spread four slices of bread with mayonnaise to taste. Layer each with a slice of lettuce, an egg foo yung patty, a tomato slice, and pickles (optional). Cover with remaining slices of bread and serve immediately.

Yield: 4 sandwiches

NOTE: Onion rolls are a delicious nontraditional substitute for white bread.

Montana has a long history of cattle ranching. Following the defeat of the Plains Indians, large herds of cattle were driven into the area, and by the early 1860s, cattlemen controlled enormous landholdings acquired by a squatter's rights law called "customary range." Today, Montana's largest industry is agriculture, with 49 percent contributed by livestock. In fact, cows outnumber people in the state three to one. It's no wonder, then, that beef is king on Montana's dining tables. Visitors and locals alike favor steak houses and old-fashioned road-houses that serve up plenty of beef along with another Montana specialty, buffalo. Burgers, beef or buffalo, are favored at lunch, while steaks are a star attraction for dinner.

FIRST NEWSPAPER   MONTANA   TERRITORY   VIRGINIA CITY, MONTANA

In Gardiner, Montana, the original north entrance to Yellowstone National Park, Helen Gould gets virtually slammed with customers throughout the summer tourist season. Since she opened the Corral Drive Inn, also fondly known as Helen's Corral, in 1960, Helen has sold about one-and-a-half million of her legendary half-pound burgers. The choices are two: beef or buffalo meat. Buffalo burgers are delicious, but because they're lower in fat than beef, they must be cooked at a lower heat, and they're generally served rare or medium.

There are plenty of Montana restaurants that serve excellent steaks, but, surprisingly, steak sandwiches are few and far between. Nevertheless, if one wants to enjoy Montana steak in a place with great atmosphere, the place to go is the Road Kill Café, about fifteen miles south of Big Timber. A small, rustic eatery established back in the 1940s, the café's motto is "From Your Grill to Ours," a tongue-in-cheek bit of humor backed by big, grilled, meltingly tender, hand-cut rib-eye steaks. There's fine eating here, Montana-style, with sides of cheddar mashed potatoes, awesome beer-battered french fries, and "bear scat" (breaded and deep-fried cheddar cheese), all washed down with Moose Drool, a brown ale produced by the Big Sky Brewing Company in Missoula. Actor Michael Keaton and newscaster Tom Brokaw, who both own ranches in the area, frequently dine anonymously at the Road Kill Café, unrecognized by local cattlemen, hardworking folks who seldom go to the movies or watch national TV. On the weekends, the old jukebox is cranked up, and locals teach guests from nearby dude ranches how to dance country-style. Keaton and Brokaw have yet to be spotted on the dance floor.

BUFFALO BURGERS

Olive oil

1 pound buffalo meat, ground

Kosher salt and fresh ground pepper to taste

2 quality hamburger rolls

Condiments of choice, such as mustard, ketchup, relish, and onion

WHERE TO GO:

Corral Drive Inn (Helen's Corral) (seasonal)
Highway 89
Gardiner, MT 59030
(406) 848-7627

Road Kill Café
Highway 298 (15 $1/2$ miles south of Big Timber)
Big Timber, MT 59011
(406) 932-6174

NEED A QUICK FIX?

Buffalo meat will be shipped anywhere in the United States from:

Montana-Wyoming Buffalo Company
Box 1503
Chinook, MT 59523
(406) 357-2611
(866) 861-0374 toll free
www.mont-wy-buffalo.com

PREHEAT AN OUTDOOR GRILL, and brush the grid lightly with olive oil to keep burgers from sticking during cooking. Loosely form the ground buffalo meat into two half-pound patties, and season each side of the burgers with salt and pepper to taste. Lower grill heat to medium-low and place burgers on the grill away from direct flames. Cook them slowly until they are brown on one side and partially cooked, about 6 to 8 minutes, then turn and cook about 6 minutes longer. Watch the burgers carefully since they will cook faster than beef due to their lower fat content. Buffalo burgers are best when grilled rare or medium. Remove burgers from the grill, place on hamburger rolls, and serve with condiments of choice.

Yield: 2 sandwiches

CHEESE FRENCHEE

This recipe is adapted from several traditional Cheese Frenchee recipes.

BATTER:

3/4 cup all-purpose flour

1 teaspoon salt

1 egg, lightly beaten

1 cup milk

IN A LARGE SHALLOW BOWL, mix flour and salt. Combine egg with milk and add to flour mixture, whisking until batter is smooth. Set aside.

WHERE TO GO:

Jimmy Aces Platinum Grill
913 South Street
Lincoln, NE 68502
(402) 475-4669

SANDWICH:

8 slices white sandwich bread

Mayonnaise

Mustard (optional)

4 thin slices American cheese

4 thin slices Swiss or Monterey Jack cheese

Oil or vegetable shortening for deep-frying

1 (7-ounce) box cornflakes, finely crushed

Batter (see left)

Ketchup (optional)

LAY OUT 4 SLICES of bread and spread lightly with mayonnaise and mustard, if desired. Top each piece of bread with a slice of American cheese and a slice of Swiss or Monterey Jack cheese. Cover each with a second slice of bread and lightly press the sandwiches together.

In a deep 12-inch frying pan, heat oil or shortening of 1 inch deep to 350 degrees. Place the crushed

Howdy from NEBRASKA

Punching Cattle on a Jack Rabbit

The Frenchee, a Nebraska favorite, was the creation of the King's Food Host Restaurants. A trademark was filed for the term Frenchee by Food Host U.S.A., Inc. of Lincoln, Nebraska, listing the date of first use as 1955. King's apparently closed sometime around the early 1970s, but eventually the sandwich appeared on the menus of other Nebraska restaurants, where it is also spelled Frenchie.

In 2001, Julie Buller and her son, Tom Inbody, opened Jimmy Aces Platinum Grill at 913 South Street in Lincoln, Nebraska. The restaurant is located on the site of the old King's Food Host, and they serve an authentic, homemade cheese Frenchee. Julie reports that the sandwich was included on the menu in response to popular demand from area patrons. On occasion, Jimmy Aces also offers the tuna Frenchee as a special.

While sources and recipes differ, the basic cheese Frenchee is an artery-clogging sandwich craved by many folks who enjoyed it in their youth. It's made with white sandwich bread (some say it had three layers of bread) spread with salad dressing or mayonnaise (the addition of mustard is optional) and filled with Swiss, American or Monterey Jack cheese (or any combination thereof). The sandwich is then batter-dipped, sometimes rolled in cornflakes, and either fried or deep-fried until golden. It is occasionally served with ketchup or seafood cocktail sauce, making the sandwich an odd imitation of the Monte Cristo, which is dipped in jam. The tuna Frenchee is filled with tuna salad and prepared in the same manner.

cornflakes in a shallow bowl or pie plate. Dip the first sandwich in batter to lightly but completely cover, then dip it in the cornflake crumbs. Repeat with the second sandwich, then carefully add both sandwiches to the hot oil. Deep-fry the sandwiches until golden brown on the first side, then carefully turn them, using two spatulas, and continue to fry until golden brown on the second side. Remove and drain on paper towels while repeating with the remaining two sandwiches. Slice each sandwich in quarters and serve with ketchup if desired.

Yield: 4 sandwiches

NOTE: Although certainly not traditional, the addition of 2 or 3 slices of crisply fried bacon and/or 2 thin slices of fresh tomato creates an excellent variation of the Frenchee.

The Basques originally traveled to the American West seeking their fortunes during Gold Rush days, but it wasn't long before they turned their attention to sheepherding. Since 1870, Basques have lived in northern Nevada, and many operated boardinghouses and hotels that catered to the sheepherders when they came into town. Several of those hotel dining rooms are still in operation, serving family-style dinners.

Over the years, Nevada Basques have strived to retain their foodways, and if one is lucky enough, delicious specialties can be uncovered in the region. One such specialty is chorizo, a spicy pork sausage, and there's none better than that made by Pete and Martha Coscarart at Villa Basque Deli in Carson City, Nevada. A friendly, unassuming man, Pete grew up on a farm in Azpilcueta in Navarre, Spain, before coming to America in 1970. His chorizo is handmade from 100 percent quality pork shoulder, and it's 85 percent fat-free. Butterflied and char-grilled, the chorizo is plopped into a fresh French roll and topped with chopped mild green Ortega chilies and Spanish pimientos, creating a feast for the eyes as well as the taste buds. The chorizo special comes complete with Basque baked beans that also contain a judicious amount of Pete's famous chorizo.

Although Villa Basque doesn't currently ship its chorizo, it is sold from the deli case by the pound. Customers can also buy Pete and Martha's homemade chorizo tamales (pork and chicken are available, too, and beef tamales can be specials ordered) plus cans of those unique sweet Spanish pimientos.

WHERE TO GO:

Villa Basque Deli
730 Basque Way
Carson City, Nevada 89706
(775) 884-4451

Villa Basque Deli's
Chorizo Sausage Sandwich

Reprinted with permission from
Villa Basque Deli, Carson City, Nevada

1 quality Spanish chorizo, butterflied

1 (6-inch) sweet French roll

Mild green Ortega chilies, chopped

Spanish pimientos, chopped

CHAR-GRILL THE CHORIZO at medium-high heat until cooked through and browned. Place chorizo in the roll, top with chopped green chilies and pimientos to taste, and serve immediately.

Yield: 1 sandwich

Need a Quick Fix?

If you can't get to the Villa Basque Deli for Pete's outstanding chorizo, hot and mild versions of the Palacios brand of chorizo from Spain can be ordered from the following source:

Tienda.com
3701 Rochambeau Road
Williamsburg VA 23188
(757) 566-9606
(888) 472-1022 toll free
www.tienda.com

CELEBRITY SANDWICH'S MONTEREY RANCH PANINI

Reprinted with permission from Dott Ferrari, founder and owner
of Celebrity Sandwich, Portsmouth, New Hampshire

8 slices Focaccia or other rustic-style
Italian bread

1/2 cup prepared ranch dressing

4 (4-ounce) boneless chicken breast
halves, grilled and thinly sliced

16 slices fresh tomato

16 slices bacon, fried crisp and drained

4 slices Monterey Jack cheese, or enough
to completely cover the sandwich

Olive oil (extra virgin is recommended)

LAY OUT THE BREAD and spread the inside
of each slice with 1 tablespoon of Ranch dressing. Cover each of four slices of bread with one
of the sliced chicken breast halves, 4 tomato
slices, 4 slices of bacon, and 1 slice of
Monterey Jack cheese. Cover with remaining
4 slices of bread. Brush the top and bottom of
each sandwich with olive oil for flavor and to
prevent sticking while cooking.

Panini can be cooked on an indoor-style grill, a
stovetop grill, a panini grill, or by using two very
large frying pans. For the stovetop method, place
the panini in one of the frying pans and place a
slightly smaller, heavy pan on top of the panini to
weight them down. Cook over medium heat for
4 minutes, turn the panini over, replace the second frying pan, and cook for 4 more minutes,
or until the bread is toasted and the filling is
warmed through. Remove from pan, slice, and
serve immediately.

Yield: 4 sandwiches

NOTE: Ciabatta is excellent for this sandwich; you'll
need 2 (13 x 5-inch) ciabattas, each cut into 4 equal
pieces. Slice off a bit of the interior from each side to
thin it down somewhat, reserving the center of the
bread for another use. Marinate the chicken breasts in
Italian dressing for 2 hours, refrigerated, then grill until
they reach an internal temperature of 160 degrees.

New Hampshire made the American sandwich scene big time when Portsmouth-native Dott Ferrari returned to her hometown and opened Celebrity Sandwich in 1989. Dott had lived for several years in California, where she frequented a restaurant that named its sandwiches after film celebrities, and she decided that a similar business would be a great idea in Portsmouth, too. Dott's idea was a resounding success, and today, Celebrity Sandwich offers 125 star-studded creations, all named after a host of famous people that reads like a "Who's Who" in film and television.

The latest additions to Celebrity's menu are panini, an Americanization of the Italian word panino, which means "little sandwich." Panini became popular in the United States in the late 1990s. They are said to have originated in Lombardy, Italy, in response to the demand among Milanese office workers for a quick lunch without sacrifice in flavor or quality. In both Italy and the United States, panini are eaten for lunch and as snacks and appetizers. In Italy, sandwich shops tradition-

JACOB'S LADDER, MT. WASHINGTON RAILWAY, WHITE MOUNTAINS, N. H.

ally wrap the bottom of the panino in a crisp white paper napkin, providing a practical solution to drips while enhancing the aesthetics.

Quality Italian bread is an absolute must for a killer panini, and most sandwich chefs will opt for a relatively thin artisan bread like focaccia or ciabatta, slicing it in half horizontally. Panini are always grilled, so most restaurants and cafés have invested in professional grooved sandwich presses that flatten and heat the sandwich while creating a crunchy, buttery outer crust. Although electric panini grills for the home are now commonly available, many cooks make do with two heated skillets: the sandwich is placed in the bottom pan and the top pan is lightly pressed down on the panini. Either way, the result is a whole new dimension added to the traditional concept of the American grilled-cheese sandwich.

WHERE TO GO:

Celebrity Sandwich
171 Islington Street
Portsmouth, NH 03801
(603) 433-7009
www.celebritysandwich.com

"Taylor Ham" is a major food group in the state of New Jersey. Actually, it's a pork roll that is now sold by several firms, but Taylor Provisions in Trenton, New Jersey, is said to have created the original product. Regardless of manufacturer, folks in Jersey insist upon calling it "Taylor Ham" even though the government seems to have stepped in at some point in time and said it was illegal to sell it as "ham." New Jersey expatriates scattered throughout the United States pine for it, and they unashamedly beg friends and relatives back home to ship a "fix" to them every so often.

It's no secret that folks in the New Jersey area continually seek out the best place for a fried "Taylor Ham" sandwich, whether for breakfast (usually with eggs) or lunch, when it's typically served on a hamburger bun or Kaiser roll with melted cheese. Holly Moore, an authority on great sandwiches and creator of www.HollyEats.com, has been known to ferret out some of the best sandwich joints in the country. For Taylor Ham, or pork roll sandwiches, Holly recommends Weber's Drive-In, an old-fashioned restaurant serving real Weber's root beer in Pennsauken, New Jersey. Here, Taylor pork roll is served on a soft hamburger bun with cheese, and patrons wash it down with a frosty mug of Weber's root beer. Carhops complete the ambiance.

With My Pals on the Beach, Ocean Grove, N. J.

NEW JERSEY–STYLE PORK ROLL (AKA TAYLOR HAM) SANDWICH

2 tablespoons butter

4 thin slices pork roll (Taylor Ham), slit a couple of times around the edge to prevent curling

1 slice American cheese

1 hamburger bun or Kaiser roll, warmed

MELT BUTTER in a medium frying pan. Add pork roll slices and fry over medium heat just until they begin to brown. Push the pork slices together a bit to bunch them up in the pan and lay the American cheese on top. Cover and cook a minute longer, or until the cheese melts. Immediately place pork slices and cheese on the bun and serve.

Yield: 1 sandwich

NOTE: Fried onions make a tasty topping for this sandwich.

WHERE TO GO:

Weber's Drive-In (seasonal)
Route 38 and King Road
Pennsauken, NJ 08110
(856) 662-6632

NEED A QUICK FIX?

There's now help for folks suffering from a craving for Taylor Pork Roll (a.k.a. Taylor Ham.). It can be purchased on the Internet at www.porkrollxpress.com and shipped fresh to your door. In addition to the Taylor (original) brand, two others are available: Kohler and Trenton.

NEW MEXICAN TOSTADAS COMPUESTAS

Adapted from Cocinas de New Mexico, Public Service Company of New Mexico (1994)

TOSTADAS:

8 corn tortillas

4 cups chile con carne (see right)

2 to 3 cups grated cheddar cheese, to taste

1/2 cup chopped green onion

2 cups coarsely chopped lettuce

2 cups coarsely chopped fresh tomatoes

Vegetable oil for frying

IN A DEEP MEDIUM-SIZE FRYING PAN, add oil to a depth of 2 inches and heat until it just begins to smoke. Fry corn tortillas one at a time, depressing in the middle with tongs to form a shallow cup. Drain on paper towels.

Preheat broiler at medium-high heat. Fill each tortilla cup with 1/2 cup chile con carne and top with grated cheddar to taste. Place tortilla cups on a baking sheet and place under broiler just long enough to melt the cheese. Remove from broiler, top with onion, lettuce, and tomatoes, and serve immediately.

Yield: 8 tostadas

CHILE CON CARNE:

1 1/2 pounds ground beef

3/4 cup chopped onion

3 cloves fresh garlic, finely chopped

1 (15-ounce) can tomato sauce

1 (15 1/2-ounce) can (about 1 1/2 cups) pinto beans, drained and rinsed

1 teaspoon kosher salt

2 tablespoons pure hot New Mexico chile powder, or 2 to 4 tablespoons pure mild New Mexico chile powder, to taste

2 cups beef broth or water

IN A DEEP MEDIUM-SIZE FRYING PAN, sauté the ground beef and onion over medium heat until the meat loses its pink color and the onions are softened. Add garlic the last minute of cooking. Drain off fat, return the mixture to the pan, and add remaining ingredients, mixing well. Cook over medium-high heat, stirring occasionally, for 30 minutes, or until most of the liquid has evaporated and the mixture is thick. Set aside and keep warm.

WHERE TO GO:

La Posta de Mesilla
2410 Calle de San Albino
Mesilla, NM 88046
(505) 524-3524
www.laposta-de-mesilla.com

NEED A QUICK FIX?

Hatch, New Mexico, is the "Chile Capital of the World." Hatch Chile Express offers genuine New Mexico chiles, including pure red chile powder.

Hatch Chile Express
P.O. Box 350
Hatch, NM 87937
(800) 292-4454 toll free
www.hatch-chile.com

While the usual sandwiches can be found in New Mexico, visitors seeking great food really need to "think out of the box." Here, the sandwich can take on a whole new meaning. Consider, for example, tamales, tostadas, tacos, flautas, and burritos, which are actually a Southwest version of the sandwich. Depending upon the individual preparation, they can be eaten out of hand or from a plate with knife and fork.

In Mesilla, New Mexico, tourists and locals alike flock to La Posta, a Mexican-style restaurant established in 1939 in a building that once served as a way station for stagecoaches operating along the Butterfield Overland Mail Route. La Posta's compound, now more than 185 years old, is on the National Register of Historic Places. The menu offers a sizable choice of New Mexican specialties based on a unique blend of Indian and Hispanic cooking, and portions are generous. A specialty of the house since 1939 is the Tostada Compuesta, corn tortilla boats filled with beans (frijoles) and red chile con carne, then topped off with lettuce, tomato, and grated cheddar cheese. The standard sauces tend to be mild, but those with a preference for more heat can request extra-spicy selections.

Times Building, New York.

The origin of the Reuben sandwich, composed of corned beef, Swiss cheese, and sauerkraut, is a hotly contested issue involving at least three separate camps. The first story is based in New York City, where it's claimed that Arnold Reuben, a German emigrant, created it in 1914. Actress Anna Seelos asked for a large sandwich when she came into Reuben's original delicatessen after her nightly performance because she was so hungry, and Reuben created a big combo sandwich that the actress devoured on the spot. However, that sandwich was composed of rye bread, baked Virginia ham, roast turkey, Swiss cheese, coleslaw, and Reuben's special Russian dressing, and it was called the "Reuben Special." Reuben's son, Arnold, Jr., said that years later, in the 1930s, a chef at the family restaurant named Alfred Schueing layered corned beef onto toasted dark pumpernickel bread and added cheese and sauerkraut, all the basic components of the sandwich that we know today as the Reuben. Arnold Reuben himself was wont to brag that his business had progressed from "a schtoonky delicatessen" to a nice restaurant and "from a sandwich to an institution."

An opposing claim comes from Omaha, Nebraska, where it's said that Reuben Kulakofsky, a grocer and owner of the Central Market, created a sandwich of corned beef, Swiss cheese, and sauerkraut on rye bread in the early 1920s for hungry, late-night poker players at the Blackstone Hotel. The sandwich was so well received that Charles Schimmel, owner of the hotel, put it on the menu and named it the Reuben in honor of its creator. In 1956, Fern Snider, a former waitress at the Blackstone, won a national sandwich competition with the recipe for the Reuben.

And then there is a third claim that the Reuben originated at the Cornhusker Hotel in Lincoln, Nebraska, in 1937. Supporting this theory is a menu from that same year listing the Reuben with its traditional ingredients. As of this writing, menus substantiating the other two claims have not yet publicly surfaced. Nevertheless, New Yorkers have embraced the Reuben, and nowhere is a finer sandwich served than at New York City's many famous delicatessens.

Corned beef, usually made from beef brisket, is beef that has been "corned," or cured in salt. Pastrami is also made from beef that has been cured in salt brine, but it involves a second step whereby the meat is smoked over hardwood sawdust.

Today, the Reuben sandwich is usually composed of thinly sliced corned beef, Swiss cheese, sauerkraut, and Russian dressing piled between slices of rye bread and quickly grilled, resulting in a sandwich that is hot on the outside and cool within. In New York, sides of coleslaw and kosher dill pickles traditionally accompany the Reuben.

THE NEW YORK REUBEN

This is actually a mini version of the Reuben sold at New York City delis, where a single sandwich is so large it can easily feed two people.

RUSSIAN DRESSING:

2 tablespoons sweet pickle relish

1 tablespoon ketchup

2 tablespoons mayonnaise

A dash of Louisiana-style hot sauce

COMBINE ALL ingredients, mixing well. Store, covered, in the refrigerator until ready to use.

Yield: enough for 4 or 5 Reuben sandwiches

SANDWICH:

2 slices of quality Jewish rye bread

Butter

$1/4$ pound thinly sliced corned beef

2 ounces thinly sliced Swiss cheese

1 tablespoon Russian dressing (see left)

$1/4$ cup sauerkraut

BUTTER ONE SIDE of each slice of bread. Place the first slice, buttered side down, in a frying pan. Pile on the slices of corned beef and Swiss cheese, spread with Russian dressing, and add the sauerkraut. Top with another slice of bread, buttered side up. Cover and grill slowly over low heat for 5 minutes, or until the bread is toasted golden brown. Uncover, turn the sandwich over, increase heat to medium high, and grill until golden brown on the second side. Cut sandwich in half and serve immediately with kosher dills or "half sours" (partially dilled pickles).

Yield: 1 sandwich

WHERE TO GO:

There's nothing like a New York deli for traditional sandwiches made from hand-carved corned beef and pastrami. Katz's Deli, founded in 1888, is the oldest and largest. The movie *When Harry Met Sally* was filmed there, and Katz's is also known for its creation of the famous World War II advertising slogan "Send a salami to your boy in the army." The sign still hangs in the restaurant. Katz's is located in Manhattan's Lower East Side, the historic neighborhood where many immigrant Jews first lived after arriving in America. Once home to pushcart peddlers, the area is a terrific source of traditional Jewish foods like bagels, bialys, and excellent deli meats. The Second Avenue Deli, founded in Manhattan's Lower East Side in 1954, is kosher and a favorite neighborhood eating spot still relatively unknown among tourists. Two other famous delicatessens, Carnegie and Stage, are located in Midtown Manhattan, and they offer table as well as counter service. All four delis are known for the great sour and half-sour pickles that accompany their sandwiches and for the ambiance provided by brusque countermen who fill orders at top speed and who expect patrons to quickly belt out their orders.

Katz's Delicatessen
205 East Houston Street
New York, NY 10002
(212) 254-2246
www.katzdeli.com

Carnegie Delicatessen
854 Seventh Avenue
New York, NY 10019
(212) 757-3012
(800) 334-5606 toll free
www.carnegiedeli.com

Stage Delicatessen
834 Seventh Avenue
New York, NY 10019
(212) 245-7850
www.stagedeli.com

Second Avenue Deli
156 Second Avenue
New York, NY 10003
(212) 677-0606
(800) 692-3354 toll free
www.2ndavedeli.com

CAMPING IN THE ADIRONDACKS, N. Y.

NEED A QUICK FIX?

Pastrami and corned beef—
When nothing else will do, New York's four most famous delis will ship their pastrami and corned beef. Carnegie will also ship sandwiches, and the mail-order menu from Second Avenue Deli is staggering. Just call them to order.

Real deli-style pickles—
No self-respecting Jewish-style deli would forego serving really great pickles. Half-sours are also known as "half-done" pickles, and they taste like a crunchy, garlicky cucumber. And then there are the half-sour tomatoes (green tomatoes that are soaked in pickling brine). If you can't get to the legendary Gus's Pickles in New York City's Lower East Side, help is now available. The enterprising owners of Pickle-Licious teamed up with Gus's, and they'll ship both half-sour pickles and tomatoes.

Pickle-Licious
(201) 836-7800
www.picklelicious.com

NORTH CAROLINA

North Carolina's turkey industry is one of the largest in the country. Production of some 41 million turkeys brings in $475 million annually to the state's economy, and the turkey is celebrated at the North Carolina Turkey Festival, held the third full weekend in September, in Raeford. At the Turkey Hoagie Brunch, visitors enthusiastically gobble up Tar Heel Turkey Hoagies made from gilled turkey tenderloins.

Historic New Bern, North Carolina, is a popular tourist destination. More than 150 of the city's homes and buildings are on the National Register of Historic Places. It's also the birthplace of Pepsi Cola, created by pharmacist Caleb D. Bradham in the late 1890s. Although Bradham's first drugstore no longer exists, his second pharmacy, built around 1912, is now home to The Chelsea, a restaurant that serves up a good helping of Southern hospitality and a tasty roster of sandwiches, many of which feature North Carolina turkey. One of the best, and a favorite of Chelsea patrons, is Chef Shawn Hoveland's Garlic Parmesan Deli Hoagie featuring turkey, salami, tomato, red onion, and olive relish. This delicious combination may well replace the Muffaletta in the hearts of sandwich fans everywhere.

GARLIC PARMESAN DELI HOAGIE

Reprinted with permission from Chef Shawn Hoveland, The Chelsea,
New Bern, North Carolina

OLIVE RELISH:

4 cups or 1 (21-ounce) jar Spanish (Manzanilla) olives stuffed with pimiento, drained

1 cup small pitted ripe (black) olives, drained

1 tablespoon olive oil

3 tablespoons chopped fresh garlic

1 tablespoon sugar

2 tablespoons red wine vinegar

PULSE THE OLIVES in a food processor until finely chopped, then set aside. In a small frying pan, heat the olive oil over medium heat and sauté the garlic just until it begins to turn a very light golden brown, about 2 minutes. Mix the garlic with the remaining ingredients, place in a large glass jar, cover tightly, and refrigerate until ready to use.

Yield: 4 cups

GARLIC PARMESAN HOAGIE ROLLS:

1 bulb fresh garlic

Olive oil

1 cup butter, softened

Freshly grated Parmesan cheese

6 10-inch hoagie rolls

PREHEAT OVEN to 350 degrees. Cut the bulb of garlic in half and place it on a large square of aluminum foil. Sprinkle lightly with olive oil, wrap tightly, and place in the oven for 45 minutes to 1 hour, until the garlic is roasted and softened. Remove from oven, let cool slightly, and then remove garlic from its husks. Add roasted garlic to the softened butter, mixing well. Slice open the hoagie rolls and spread each side with 1 heaping tablespoon of the garlic butter. Preheat broiler and place the open hoagie rolls on a baking sheet. Sprinkle lightly with freshly grated Parmesan cheese and broil until golden brown.

Yield: 1 cup garlic butter or enough for 6 hoagie rolls

SANDWICH:

1 (10-inch) garlic Parmesan hoagie roll (see left)

4 ounces thinly sliced roasted turkey breast

4 ounces thinly sliced Genoa salami

3 leaves lettuce

3 thin slices beefsteak tomato

3 to 6 rings thinly sliced red onion, or more to taste

2 tablespoons olive relish, or more to taste (see left page)

ON THE BOTTOM HALF of the hoagie roll, layer the turkey, salami, lettuce, tomato, and red onion. Top with olive relish, cover with top half of the roll, and slice in half. Serve immediately.

Yield: 1 sandwich

NOTE: The olive relish is delicious and definitely addictive—you may well wish to add more than the 2 tablespoons called for above. Leftover olive relish keeps well in the refrigerator when tightly covered; it's a great enhancement to many other sandwich combinations.

WHERE TO GO: The Chelsea
335 Middle Street
New Bern, NC 28560
(252) 637-5469
www.thechelsea.com

In Kansas, folks favor handheld meat pies called bierocks while their neighbors in Nebraska prefer krautranzen, sold as Runzas® by a locally headquartered restaurant chain. But in North Dakota, settled early on by Black Sea Germans from Russia, the specialty of choice is fleischkuechle [fly-sh-keeK-la] (fleisch translates as "meat" and kuechle as "dough" or "bread"). Little-known outside the region, fleischkuechle are composed of meat that's seasoned, encased in dough, and then deep-fried to a rich golden crispness. One is tempted to refer to them as North Dakota's version of the all-American hamburger.

As has occurred with many of America's heritage foods, homemade fleischkuechle are becoming more and more rare, especially in restaurants where visitors to North Dakota would be most likely to find them. Many establishments have adopted commercially prepared versions, those cafés that still offer freshly made fleischkuechle to the public are to be revered indeed.

One such eating establishment is the Dairy Queen in the tiny town of Beulah, North Dakota. Here, Betty Mae Hausauer has reigned supreme in the kitchen for some twenty years, single-handedly making anywhere between 100 and 250 fleischkeuchle per day, depending on the season. Most diners top off their fleischkeuchle with pickles and ketchup. Locals, visitors, and those who were born and raised in North Dakota but now make their home elsewhere flock to the Dairy Queen in search of Betty Mae's fleischkeuchle, and most buy several boxes to take back to places like Texas and California. Betty Mae, who treasures traditional foodways and seeks to preserve them, is rightfully proud of the fact that she provides so many people with a true taste of North Dakota.

WHERE TO GO:

Dairy Queen
1300 Highway 49 North
Beulah, ND 58523
(701) 873-2555

DOUGH:

1 egg, lightly beaten

1 cup half-and-half or canned milk

1 cup milk

1 tablespoon vegetable oil

5 cups (approximately) all-purpose flour

1 teaspoon salt

IN A LARGE BOWL, combine egg, canned milk or half-and-half, milk, and oil and mix well. Sift together the flour and salt and mix into the liquids to make a smooth dough. Add additional flour if necessary. Let dough rest while preparing filling.

FILLING:

2 pounds ground beef

1 teaspoon salt, or to taste

1/2 teaspoon black pepper, or to taste

Half of a large onion, finely chopped

1/2 cup water to make filling spreadable

PLACE ALL INGREDIENTS in a bowl and mix well.

FLEISCHKUECHLE

Reprinted with permission from Betty Mae Hausauer of the Dairy Queen, Beulah, North Dakota

SANDWICH:

Dough (see left)

Filling (see below left)

Vegetable oil for frying

Pickles

Ketchup

DIVIDE DOUGH into 10 small balls about the size of lemons. On a well-floured board, roll out each piece of dough to a diameter of 12 inches. Divide meat filling into 10 equal portions. Thinly spread a portion of meat filling on half of each piece of dough, fold the other half of the dough over the filling, and seal the edges well by tightly pressing with a fork. On one side, prick the fleischkeuchle twice with a fork to allow steam to escape while cooking. Repeat with remaining dough and filling.

In a deep 12-inch frying pan, add vegetable oil to a depth of 1 inch, and heat it to 350 degrees. Carefully add the fleischkeuchle and fry, one at a time, until deep golden brown on both sides. Drain on paper towels and serve hot, accompanied by ketchup and pickles.

Yield: 10 fleischkeuchle

NOTE: The amount of black pepper may be increased to 1 1/2 teaspoons. The addition of 2 large cloves of garlic, finely chopped, delivers a delicious but nontraditional variation.

THE HIPPO

Reprinted with permission from Price Hill Chili, Cincinnati, Ohio

Mayonnaise (cholesterol-free)

3 slices bread (white, whole wheat, or dark rye), toasted

4 ounces thinly sliced roast beef

2 large thin slices American or Swiss cheese

3 thin slices fresh tomato

4 ounces thinly sliced (99 percent fat-free) smoked ham

2 leaves iceberg lettuce

Extra-long toothpicks

SPREAD MAYONNAISE on one side of each slice of bread. Lay out a slice of bread and top with roast beef and cheese. Place another slice of bread on top, and add tomato slices, ham, and lettuce. Top with remaining slice of bread, cut sandwich in half, insert a toothpick in each half to hold it together, and serve immediately.

Yield: 1 sandwich

Ohio is the land of the double-decker sandwich. It's similar to a club sandwich but dwarfs it in size. Actually, the double-decker makes many hoagies and subs look like mere appetizers.

Cincinnati, Ohio, is known for its chili parlors that serve a chili unique to the area. Many of these restaurants are located in the west-side neighborhood of Price Hill, and they also serve double-deckers, but it's Price Hill Chili that has earned special accolades for its sandwiches. Founded by Sam Beltsos and his father-in-law, Lazaros Nourtsis, Price Hill Chili is a local icon and popular meeting spot for politicians and west-side families, and its enormous sandwiches are legendary. The Landmark is a belly-busting combination of Salisbury steak, onions, bacon, and mayonnaise, and The Big Sam consists of two cheeseburgers topped with onion, lettuce, tomato and a healthy scoop of coleslaw. But it's the Hippo that has become the most popular double-decker sandwich at Price Hill Chili, and thanks to Sam Beltsos, a personable and generous host, the recipe is provided here for all to enjoy.

WHERE TO GO:

Price Hill Chili
4920 Glenway Avenue
Cincinnati, OH 45238
(513) 471-9507

New West Side Market House, Cleveland Sixth City

It's no secret that Oklahomans love their beef, and they're likely to enjoy charbroiled steaks as much as that regional Southwest favorite, chicken fried steak. In Bartlesville, Oklahoma, known as "the town that oil built," due to its association with Frank Phillips, founder of Phillips 66, a huge neon Hereford advertising Murphy's Original Steak House beckons diners in search of great steak. Murphy's was established back in 1946, and it's still going strong.

But there's a surprise in store for first-time visitors to Murphy's. First of all, Murphy's is known for its gravy-drenched french fries. And although the steaks are great, a close look at neighboring tables will reveal an interesting dish billed on the menu as the Hot Hamburger. It's an architectural wonder of the culinary world, built to towering perfection from a foothold of toasted white bread followed by consecutive stories of french fries, a beef patty judiciously hacked into bite-size pieces drenched in rich beef gravy, and capped with fried onions. The contented looks on diners' faces tell the rest of the story.

The Hot Hamburger is reminiscent of horseshoe and pony-shoe sandwiches, specialties of Springfield, Illinois; the difference lies in a topping of gravy and fried onions versus cheese sauce. Although the preparation of Murphy's Hot Hamburger is a trade secret, the following instructions provide a reasonable duplication for those finding themselves in need of a quick fix.

HOT HAMBURGER

as served at Murphy's Original Steak House

3 tablespoons butter or oil

3 large yellow onions, thinly sliced

1 cup beef gravy (see page 113)

1 pound ground beef shaped into 2 (1/2-pound) burgers

4 cups shoestring-style frozen french fries

2 slices white bread, toasted

WHERE TO GO:

Murphy's Original Steak House
1625 SW Frank Phillips Boulevard
Bartlesville, OK 74003
(918) 336-4789

IN A MEDIUM FRYING PAN, heat butter or oil, add the onions and fry over medium heat until they are soft and golden brown. Prepare gravy and keep warm. Grill or fry the hamburgers to desired degree of doneness, and heat the french fries in the oven according to package directions. Just before the burgers and fries are done, toast the bread and place 1 slice of toast on each of 2 plates. Remove fries from oven and place half on each slice of toast. Cut each burger into bite-size pieces and place on top of fries. Ladle 1/2 cup of gravy over each serving, top each with half the fried onions, and serve immediately.

Yield: 2 servings

DOOGER'S DUNGENESS CRAB CAKE SANDWICH

**Reprinted with permission from Dooger's Seafood & Grill,
Cannon Beach, Oregon**

Oregon is known for its wonderful fresh seafood, especially oysters, razor clams, and delectable Dungeness crabs. The latter has been a mainstay of Oregon's seafaring industry since the late 1800s. Oregon fishermen, creating a significant contribution to the state's economy, land an average annual catch of around 10 million pounds.

Visitors to Oregon frequently head for Cannon Beach, a seaside community known for its art galleries and gift shops. The town is named for a cannon that washed ashore from the USS Shark, which was shipwrecked in 1846. While there are plenty of attractions in Cannon Beach, one of the favorite "sports" is eating, and in their quest for great Oregon seafood, most folks eventually head for Dooger's Seafood & Grill. Established in 1983, there are two additional locations in Seaside and Long Beach. A favorite from the sandwich menu is the Dungeness Crab Cake Sandwich, a lovely open-face sandwich topped with hollandaise sauce. Dooger's is also known for its clam chowder, so popular that they sell "chowder kits" by mail order to customers as far away as Europe and Hawaii.

CRAB CAKES:

1 1/4 pounds fresh cooked Dungeness crabmeat (about 3 legs)

9 slices white bread, crusts removed

2 tablespoons butter

1/2 cup finely chopped onion

1/2 cup finely chopped celery

1 teaspoon dried basil

2 eggs, lightly beaten

1/4 cup mayonnaise

1 tablespoon Worcestershire sauce

3/4 teaspoon Tabasco sauce

2 1/2 tablespoons dried parsley

1/2 cup Panko (Japanese breadcrumbs)

1/4 cup butter

REMOVE CRABMEAT from fresh-cooked crab legs, separate it into small pieces, place in a large bowl, and set aside. Tear the bread into medium pieces, place in a food processor, and process into very fine crumbs. Add to the crabmeat; set mixture aside.

In a medium frying pan, melt butter over medium heat, add the onion, celery, and basil, and sauté the mixture over medium heat until the vegetables are softened and transparent. Add the sautéed vegetables to the crabmeat and prepared breadcrumbs, and mix well.

In a separate medium bowl, combine the eggs, mayonnaise, Worcestershire, Tabasco, and parsley, and whisk until well combined. Add to the crabmeat mixture and mix well.

Form the crabmeat mixture into 4 equal patties; if desired, cover and refrigerate the patties until ready to use. Just before cooking, gently bread the crab cakes in the Panko. In a large 12-inch frying pan, melt the butter over medium-high heat and add the crab cakes. Fry the cakes until golden brown and crispy on both sides, turning once, for about 5 to 7 minutes per side.

HOLLANDAISE SAUCE:

4 egg yolks, room temperature

6 tablespoons freshly squeezed lemon juice

1 cup very cold butter

HEAT WATER in the bottom of a double boiler until it boils, then reduce heat to low. In the top of the double boiler, combine the egg yolks and the lemon juice, mixing with a wooden spoon. Add $1/4$ cup of the butter, place top of double boiler over the bottom pan, and stir constantly until the butter melts. Repeat, adding $1/4$ cup butter at a time, until all butter has been incorporated. Continue cooking over very low heat, stirring constantly, until the sauce thickens. Remove from heat and serve hot or at room temperature.

Yield: 2 cups

A Car Load of Oregon Tomatoes.

SANDWICH:

4 slices quality white bread (or other bread of choice), toasted

Crab cakes (see page 98)

1 to 2 cups hollandaise sauce, to taste (see left)

4 lettuce leaves

4 slices fresh tomato

4 slices onion

PLACE A SLICE of toasted bread on each of four plates. Place a crab cake on each slice of bread and top with $1/4$ to $1/2$ cup of hollandaise sauce (depending upon taste). Garnish with lettuce, tomato, and onion on the side. Serve the open-faced sandwiches immediately.

Yield: 4 sandwiches

WHERE TO GO:

Dooger's Seafood & Grill
1371 South Hemlock
Cannon Beach, OR 97110
(503) 436-2225
www.cannon-beach.net/doogers

NEED A QUICK FIX?

One of Oregon's principal crab fleet homeports is Astoria. FMBSeafood, with a fleet in excess of 200 vessels, will ship Dungeness crab, live or cooked, right to your doorstep.

Fergus-Mc-Barendse (FMBSeafood)
80 - 11th Street
Astoria, OR 97103
(503) 325-9592
www.fmbseafood.org

Liberty Bell Philadelphia Pa.

According to legend, the Philadelphia cheese steak sandwich was born one day in 1930 at Pat Olivieri's hot dog stand, located at the Italian Market in south Philadelphia. Longing for something different, Olivieri cooked some thinly sliced beef and onions on his hot dog grill

In the 1940s cheese was added, and somewhere along the line Olivieri, with no competition from other vendors, declared himself "King of Steaks." Pat's only location in south Philly is still operated by the same family. It's a place where communal ties remain strong, and everyone's proud of the fact that Sylvester Stallone, also a south Philly native, filmed scenes for his first Rocky movie in the neighborhood.

The Philadelphia Cheese Steak Sandwich is composed of very thinly sliced and grilled beef and onions (rib eye steak is commonly used), hot Cheez Whiz (the most authentic), American cheese, or, more recently, provolone cheese, and usually a garnish of fried hot or sweet peppers, all piled into a crusty Italian roll. Some cheese steak emporiums chop the steak up on the grill as it cooks, creating an interesting melding of meat, onion, and cheese. Fried mushrooms, garlic, and ketchup are optional, and other additions include lettuce and tomato.

and piled it all into an Italian roll. As the story goes, a cab driver who regularly patronized the hot dog stand came by just as Pat was eating his new creation and asked for one, too. Upon tasting it, the cabbie immediately advised Pat to forget about hot dogs and sell his beef sandwich instead.

EXP. 3-31-54
1953 PENNA
7329A

THE ORIGINAL PAT'S KING OF STEAKS PHILADELPHIA CHEESE STEAK RECIPE

Reprinted with permission from Pat's King of Steaks

Cheese (Pat's recommends Cheez Whiz, but American or provolone works fine)

6 tablespoons soybean oil

1 large Spanish onion, coarsely chopped

24 ounces thinly sliced rib eye or eye roll steak

4 crusty Italian rolls

Sweet green and red peppers, coarsely chopped and sautéed in oil (optional)

Mushrooms, coarsely chopped and sautéed in oil (optional)

Ketchup (optional)

MELT THE CHEEZ WHIZ in a double boiler or in a microwave oven. Heat an iron skillet or a nonstick pan over medium heat. Add 3 tablespoons of oil to the pan, and sauté the onion to desired doneness. Remove the onion. Add the remaining oil to the skillet, and sauté the slices of meat quickly on both sides.

Place 6 ounces of the steak into each roll. Divide the onion among the rolls, and top with hot Cheez Whiz. Garnish as desired with peppers, mushrooms, and ketchup. Put on the theme song to the first Rocky movie and enjoy!

Yield: 4 sandwiches

NOTE: Steak can be sliced thinner when it is partially frozen.

WHERE TO GO:

Pat's King of Steaks
1237 East Passyunk Avenue
Philadelphia, PA 19147
(215) 468-1546
www.patskingofsteaks.com

RHODE ISLAND CLAM ROLLS

Adapted from several traditional Rhode Island clam roll recipes

TARTAR SAUCE:

3/4 cup quality mayonnaise

3 tablespoons chopped sweet pickle relish

1 tablespoon dried parsley or 2 tablespoons chopped fresh parsley

2 tablespoons finely chopped onion

2 teaspoons horseradish

IN A SMALL BOWL, combine all ingredients and mix well. Cover and refrigerate until ready to serve.

Yield: About 1 cup

NOTE: This recipe is provided courtesy of Linda Rosser of Bowmansville, New York.

BATTER:

3/4 cup evaporated milk

1 egg, lightly beaten

1/4 teaspoon Louisiana-style hot sauce, or to taste

Salt and pepper to taste

1/4 cup cake flour

3/4 cup yellow cornmeal

1/2 teaspoon celery salt

IN A MEDIUM BOWL, combine evaporated milk, egg, and hot sauce, whisking to combine thoroughly, and season to taste with salt and pepper. In a wide flat dish or pie plate, mix flour, cornmeal, and celery salt.

Seafood lovers are in for a special treat when it comes to dining in Rhode Island. The tiny Ocean State boasts more than 400 miles of coastline, and it's legendary for a large variety of quality hard-shell clams—littlenecks, cherrystones, top necks, and chowders—that are harvested in local waters. The state shell is the quahog, a clam unique to Rhode Island. The popularity of the state's clams accounts for the extraordinary number of clam shacks that dot the area, attracting locals and visitors in search of a variety of clam specialties like plain raw clams, steamed clams, clam chowder, clam cakes, clam strips, and baked clams (also called stuffies).

Clam rolls, composed of deep-fried clams served in a hot dog roll with tartar sauce and accompanied by a lemon wedge, are a popular Rhode Island treat and the subject of many hot debates relative to which clam shack serves the best to be found. Many devotees of the clam roll cast their vote in favor of those served at Flo's Clam Shack, first established in a renovated chicken coop at Portsmouth's Island Park in 1936. Despite two hurricanes that destroyed the structures in 1938 and 1991, Flo's has survived due to the tenacity of its owners and a loyal following that appreciates fresh quality seafood. A second location in Middletown was opened in 1992. Both locations are bustling operations, and a unique touch, customers waiting for takeout orders are given rocks with numbers on them. Using a top-secret recipe, Flo's clams are lightly battered and quickly deep-fried, a process that delivers crispy, tasty clams and clam rolls. Other Rhode Island clam shacks adhere to another Rhode Island tradition by breading their clams in a cornmeal mixture.

CLAMS:

Peanut oil for frying

24 whole-belly soft-shell clams, freshly shucked and well drained

Batter (see page 104)

PREHEAT OVEN to 300 degrees. In a large, deep frying pan, add peanut oil to a depth of 1 inch and heat to 375 degrees. Dip clams in the milk and egg mixture, then lightly coat with the cornmeal mixture, shaking off excess. Fry in small batches until golden brown and crisp, about 5 minutes. With a slotted spoon, remove clams to a rimmed cookie sheet lined with paper towels and set in the oven to keep warm. Repeat with remaining clams until all clams are fried.

SANDWICH:

Fried clams (see left)

6 quality hot dog rolls, lightly buttered and toasted

Tartar sauce (see page 104)

6 lemon wedges

DIVIDE FRIED CLAMS among the prepared hot dog rolls and serve immediately with tartar sauce and lemon wedges.

Yield: 6 sandwiches

OLD MAN'S FACE, NARRAGANSETT PIER, R. I.

NEED A QUICK FIX?

Champlin's will ship a large variety of clams and other Rhode Island seafood specialties.

Champlin's Seafood Market
256 Great Island Road
P.O. Box 426
Narragansett, RI 02882
(401) 783-3152
www.champlins.com

WHERE TO GO:

Flo's Clam Shack (seasonal)
4 Wave Avenue
Middletown, RI 02842
(401) 847-8141

Flo's Clam Shack (seasonal and takeout only)
Park Avenue, Island Park
Portsmouth, RI 02871

Americans love shrimp, and nowhere is this more true than in South Carolina, where **Low Country Cuisine** features it in many traditional dishes like shrimp and grits or Frogmore Stew, a seafood boil consisting of shrimp, hot smoked link sausage, and ears of fresh corn. For decades, shrimping has been a major industry in South Carolina, where the annual harvest runs between four and five million pounds. Unfortunately, demand far outstrips domestic supply, and in recent years, nearly 90 percent of the shrimp consumed in the United States has been imported. These cheap, farm-raised

ers, a specialty of the house at several casual lunch spots in the region. It's said that the best shrimp burger in the Low Country is to be had at the Shrimp Shack on St. Helena Island. Owners Bob and Hilda Upton come from a family of professional shrimpers. One of Hilda's brothers still operates a shrimp boat, while other family members are involved in Gay Fish Company, a retail market established by Hilda's parents in the 1940s, where patrons can purchase fresh South Carolina shrimp right off the boats.

The rustic Shrimp Shack, established in 1978, is located right across the road from the family shrimp docks, and the shrimp burger has always been on the menu. Hilda says that it actually originated in the 1960s as a snack made aboard the shrimp boats. Shrimp were pounded with a glass bottle, mixed with onion, and fried.

State Capitol, Columbia S. C.

The Shrimp Shack's deep-fried, ground shrimp patties are made from South Carolina shrimp, and they've garnered a loyal following in addition to nominations for the state's best seafood. Hilda's secret seasoning (which does not include onion) enhances the deep-fried patties that come in two sizes: regular and super. Most patrons want their shrimp burgers deep-fried quickly so that they're still pink in the middle, but on request, the Shrimp Shack will fry them a

competitors have had a negative impact on America's commercial shrimpers, even though many people prefer the quality of our domestic shrimp.

Numerous restaurants and food shops in South Carolina offer locally caught shrimp, much sought after by visitors and tourists alike, and dishes run from the traditional to creative items like shrimp burg-

bit longer, producing a more crispy result. They're served on hamburger buns along with mayonnaise, tartar sauce, or the Shrimp Shack special seafood cocktail sauce made with horseradish. Lettuce and tomato is optional. Hilda Upton's recipe for the shrimp burger is a closely guarded secret, but the following will do nicely if you can't get to the Shrimp Shack.

SOUTH CAROLINA-STYLE SHRIMP BURGERS

This recipe is adapted from Fred Thompson's recipe for Wonderful Shrimp Burgers, published in *The News & Observer*, Raleigh, North Carolina. Fred advocates the use of brown shrimp, found along the Mid-Atlantic coast.

COCKTAIL SAUCE:

1/3 cup quality commercial chili sauce (ketchup-style, such as Heinz)

1 tablespoon horseradish, or to taste

Dash of Louisiana-style hot sauce, or to taste

COMBINE INGREDIENTS in a small bowl, cover, and refrigerate until ready to serve.

Yield: 1/3 cup

SHRIMP BURGERS:

4 cups water

1 1/2 pounds peeled and de-veined raw shrimp with tails intact

1 3/4 cups fresh bread crumbs

1/3 cup finely chopped onion

1/3 cup finely diced celery

1 tablespoon dried parsley or 2 tablespoons chopped fresh parsley

3 tablespoons quality mayonnaise

1 egg, lightly beaten

1/2 teaspoon kosher salt

1/2 teaspoon freshly ground black pepper

1 teaspoon Louisiana-style hot pepper sauce

SHRIMP BURGERS (CON'T):

IN A LARGE SAUCEPAN, bring the water to a full boil. Add the shrimp, cover, and remove from heat for 3 minutes. Immediately cool the shrimp in a colander under cold running water and drain well. Remove tails from the shrimp. Chop 12 of the shrimp into small pieces. Place the remainder of the shrimp in a food processor fitted with a steel blade, and pulse about 6 times, or until the shrimp are light and flaky.

In a large bowl, combine all the shrimp with the bread crumbs, mixing well. Add onion, celery, and parsley, mixing well. Mix in the mayonnaise and egg, and season with salt, pepper, and hot sauce. Lightly pat the mixture into 7 (3-inch) patties, place on a platter, cover, and refrigerate for 1 hour.

SANDWICH:

2 tablespoons canola or peanut oil

7 shrimp burgers (see left)

7 hamburger buns, toasted

Cocktail sauce (see page 109) or tartar sauce (see page 104)

HEAT THE CANOLA OIL in a large non-stick frying pan to just below the smoking point. Gently add the shrimp burgers and fry them over medium heat for 3 to 4 minutes per side, or until crispy and golden brown. Place burgers on rolls and serve immediately with cocktail or tartar sauce.

Yield: 7 sandwiches

3:—MAIN STREET LOOKING NORTH FROM CAPITOL, COLUMBIA, S. C.

NEED A QUICK FIX?

Bring your own cooler and the folks at Gay Fish Company will pack it up with your personal selection of South Carolina shrimp and other seafood.

Gay Fish Company, Inc.
1948 Sea Island Parkway
St. Helena Island, SC 29220
(843) 838-2763

WHERE TO GO:

The Shrimp Shack
1929 Sea Island Parkway
St. Helena Island, SC 29920
(843) 838-2962

South Dakota is a cattle state. Like Montana, it has more cattle than people. Anyone on the prowl for good food in South Dakota needs to think beef— as in hot roast beef sandwiches covered with brown gravy and a big scoop of mashed potatoes. It's the unofficial state dish. It's also the specialty of the house at Wall Drug Store in Wall, South Dakota.

Ted and Dorothy Husted established Wall Drug in 1931. Unfortunately, tourists destined for the Black Hills and Badlands region of the state whizzed by the small store and business languished. Finally, Dorothy suggested that surely all those travelers must be thirsty, and the Husteds put up signs advertising free ice water. The marketing gimmick was a success, and business boomed. Eventually, Ted Husted saw to it that billboards advertising Wall Drug sprang up all over the country.

Today, the Wall Drug complex covers several blocks, and attracts over a million people every year. It's a kitschy mix of museum, souvenirs, and more. Free ice water is still available out in the "backyard," and at Wall Drug Café, coffee is only five cents a cup. Diners feast on the house specialty— billed as the Hot Beef—a hot roast beef sandwich on white bread with the halves separated by a scoop of mashed potatoes and covered with rich brown gravy. It's a true taste of South Dakota.

ROAST BEEF:

1 (5-pound) top round of beef roast

Ground black pepper

Garlic powder

Celery salt

PREHEAT OVEN to 450 degrees. Sprinkle the roast with pepper, garlic powder, and celery salt to taste, covering all sides. Place the roast on a rack in a baking pan and roast, uncovered, until the outside becomes brown and crispy, about 45 minutes to 1 hour. Reduce oven temperature to 325 degrees, and continue roasting until the desired degree of doneness is reached by testing with a meat thermometer. For rare, it will take about 12 minutes per pound to reach a temperature of 120 degrees, and for medium, it will take about 15 minutes per pound to reach a temperature of 140 degrees.

SOUTH DAKOTA HOT ROAST BEEF SANDWICH

Flo Piedja of Freedom, New York, prepares roast beef that would please anyone from South Dakota, and the following recipe is based on her traditional method.

BEEF GRAVY:

3 (14-ounce) cans quality beef broth

1/2 cup cold water

1/2 cup cornstarch

Browning sauce, such as Kitchen Bouquet

Salt and ground black pepper to taste

WHILE BEEF IS ROASTING, prepare the gravy. In a medium saucepan, place 2 cans of the beef broth and bring broth to a boil. In a jar or salad dressing mixer, combine the cold water and the cornstarch, shaking it well. Gradually whisk the cornstarch mixture into the boiling broth, reduce heat to medium, and let the gravy simmer for 5 minutes. Stir in enough browning sauce to give the gravy a rich, deep-brown color, and season to taste with salt and pepper. Cover and set aside.

SANDWICH:

Roast beef (see left page)

Beef gravy (see left)

12 slices quality white bread

Mashed potatoes (optional)

WHEN THE ROAST IS DONE, remove it from the oven and let it rest for 5 to 10 minutes. Reheat the gravy over medium heat, whisking in any drippings from the roast and additional beef broth to reach the desired thickness. Slice the beef very thin. For each serving, place 2 slices of white bread on a plate, separated by a scoop of mashed potatoes if desired, and cover the bread with sliced beef. Ladle hot gravy over the potatoes and beef, and serve immediately.

Yield: 6 generous servings

WHERE TO GO: Wall Drug Store
510 Main Street
Wall, SD 57790
(605) 279-2175
www.walldrug.com

Tennessee is the home of fine country cured hams and bacon. We're not talking supermarket stuff here—we're talking about the old traditional way of curing in which pork is hung in a smokehouse, producing clearly superior products that Southerners adore and that most of the rest of America has never even tasted.

Succulent Tennessee-style country cured bacon is produced today by small "boutique" businesses that an intrepid bacon lover will track down like a hound dog stalking a 'coon. There's no better bacon than that from Tripp Country Hams in Brownsville, about an hour north of Memphis. Charlie and Judy Tripp are dedicated to the business of producing quality cured hams and bacon that was started by Charlie's dad back in 1963. Not long after taking over the business, Charlie obtained a recipe from an old gentleman who dabbled in curing and sold his products at a roadside stand. The top-secret recipe, which calls for brown sugar, cinnamon, and cayenne in the dry cure, produces delicious hickory-smoked bacon second to none. Charlie's award-winning country ham and bacon business has thrived, and today it employees fifteen people.

According to Chef James Ehler of www.foodreference.com, the BLT (so named as part of diner lingo) is the second most popular sandwich in the United States (ham is number one). Thus far, research conducted by the intrepid Barry Popik has dated the term BLT to 1944 although the sandwich dates to the early 1900s.

Tripp's bacon makes the best BLT sandwich in the world, providing an added spark to traditional bacon flavor that elevates a BLT to something almost celestial with the pure porkiness of its flavor. Alas, Charlie didn't know of a restaurant that serves his bacon in a sandwich; apparently, it's just a bit too pricey in comparison to common bacon available from industry wholesalers. The only solution is to stop by the Tripp retail store or order up some bacon via their mail-order service; because it's cured, the bacon doesn't have to be refrigerated, so shipping costs are relatively inexpensive. You'll enjoy the best homemade BLT in the world.

Parthenon Centennial Park, Nashville, Tenn.

THE TENNESSEE BLTT

(Country Cured Bacon, Lettuce, Tomato, and Turkey)

Mayonnaise to taste

4 slices quality white bread, toasted

2 large leaves iceberg lettuce

1/4 cup crumbled blue cheese

2 large slices of tomato

1/4 pound very thinly sliced smoked turkey

6 slices country cured bacon (such as Tripp's), crisply cooked and drained

SPREAD MAYONNAISE on one side of each slice of toast. Lay out 2 slices of toast and cover each with a large leaf of lettuce. Divide the blue cheese between the sandwiches, then top each with a slice of tomato, half the turkey, and 3 pieces of bacon. Cover the sandwiches with the remaining slices of toast, cut in half, and serve immediately.

Yield: 2 sandwiches

WHERE TO GO:

Tripp Country Hams
P.O. Box 527
207 South Washington
Brownsville, TN 38012
(731) 772-2130
(800) 471-9814 toll-free
www.countryhams.com/tripp.htm

TEXAS-STYLE PAN-FRIED SIRLOIN

Reprinted with permission from an article by Chef David Bulla of Austin, Texas, titled "Chicken Fried Steak—A Texas Tradition Revisited" on Texas Cooking Online at www.texascooking.com

CHICKEN-FRIED STEAK:

1 teaspoon salt

1 teaspoon freshly ground black pepper

1 teaspoon granulated garlic

1 teaspoon good-quality chili powder (optional)

2 top sirloin steaks, about 1/4 inch thick (and as big as you like them), with a good marbling of fat but trimmed of fatty areas

1 cup buttermilk

1 egg

1 cup all-purpose flour

1 cup fresh bread crumbs

1 cup (more or less) vegetable oil

MIX TOGETHER THE SALT, pepper, garlic, and chili powder. Liberally season the steaks on both sides. With the coarse-spike side of a meat-tenderizing hammer, pound the seasoned steaks to tenderize them and work the seasoning into the meat. Be careful not to pound the steaks too thin, but you have to use enough force to actually start breaking down the meat fibers a little bit. Just putting a nice hammer mark on the steak won't do much. You want to make the steak a little thinner and a little larger to accomplish the tenderizing process.

In a bowl, mix the buttermilk with the egg. Set up your breading station with a bowl of flour, the bowl containing the buttermilk-egg mixture, and a bowl of bread crumbs. Dredge the steak in the flour, coating it evenly and shaking off the excess flour. Dip the steak in the buttermilk-egg mixture, then dredge the steak in the bread crumbs. Make sure the steaks are evenly coated. Set steaks aside on a plate; you can layer them between sheets of waxed paper.

If Texas has a national dish, it has got to be chicken-fried steak (CFS). Of course, it's found throughout the Southwest, and so ubiquitous is it on the menus of roadside eateries that some veteran travelers refer to Route 66, which traverses Texas from Shamrock to Glenrio, as the "Chicken Fried Steak Highway." The dish is so popular in Houston that it has sometimes been jokingly referred to as Houston Fried Steak. Texans and Houstonians both are so devoted to it that it's even served up in the form of a sandwich.

So where did chicken-fried steak originate? Most likely, its basic preparation came with settlers from the southeastern United States, who commonly prepared fried steak dishes, and from Germany, where wiener schnitzel was traditional. Both preparations called for beating steak, dredging it in flour, and then frying it. Like most recipes, they were assimilated and adapted into the developing regional food culture, eventually emerging as the chicken-fried steak known in Texas today. Some food historians date the introduction to the Depression years, when both the times and the meat were tough. From every indication, however, the dish is older than that by about a hundred years. Recent research does date coinage of the phrase "chicken-fried steak" to 1935, perhaps indicating the high cost of chicken at that time in comparison to beef.

The CFS sandwich is typically composed of a beefsteak, usually round steak about 1/2 inch thick, trimmed of fat and gristle, and tenderized. It's floured, dipped in an egg-milk batter, floured again, and plunged into a deep pan of hot fat (shortening or lard) until it's golden brown. It's served on a bun, sometimes toasted, or on Texas toast (usually white bread sliced twice as thick as normal and toasted), with a choice of condiments, including the traditional white milk or cream gravy that accompanies a CFS dinner. Other condiments of choice are cheese, mayonnaise, onion, and ketchup. Folks sometimes order the cream gravy on the side for dipping. French fries or potato chips normally accompany the sandwich.

Chef David Bulla of Austin, Texas, is on a mission to

Panhandle Bronco Buster, Dalhart, Tex.

B661A19

restore what he sees as the former glory and dignity of the chicken-fried steak. According to Bulla, a really great CFS shouldn't be delivered up in the deep-fried form that is so often found today. He advocates a return to frying the CFS in a cast-iron skillet, and he also suggests using better cuts of beef.

CHICKEN-FRIED STEAK (CON'T):

In a cast-iron skillet, heat the oil over medium heat. Have enough oil in the pan to come a little more than halfway up the side of the steaks when they are cooking. You do not want to submerge the steaks in oil. The temperature should be around 300 degrees. It will vary during the cooking process, but you want to maintain a temperature above 250 degrees and no more than about 350 degrees. Adjust the heat as necessary while you cook, maintaining a nice simmer in the pan. You will know if your pan is too hot if your steak starts to get too dark.

When the oil is hot, add the steaks. If the skillet is too small, cook them in batches. When the juices start to bleed through the top crust of the steak, turn it over. Fry about 5 minutes per side, turning the steak only once. Look for a nice brown color on the crust, like the color of dark wood but not the color of chocolate. When both sides are done, remove steak from the pan and drain on a brown paper bag or paper towels. Keep steaks in a warm oven until the gravy is ready to go.

Yield: 2 steaks or enough for 4 CFS sandwiches

Exterior View of the Buckhorn Curio Museum, San Antonio, Texas

CREAMY PAN GRAVY:

(see Chef's Note on fond)

2 tablespoons reserved oil from pan

2 tablespoons all-purpose flour

$1/4$ cup dry white wine

1 cup chicken stock

1 cup half-and-half

1 teaspoon coarsely ground fresh black pepper

1 teaspoon salt

CHEF'S NOTE: There is a term in classic French cooking called *fond*. This term describes the browned, caramelized, concentrated residue that remains in the pan after something has been cooked. The fond is what you are after when you deglaze a pan. It's what adds richness to any pan sauce. And fond is what's missing in most restaurant versions of cream gravy. The above version is a little different in that it also has chicken stock and a little wine.

FROM THE PAN you just fried your steaks in, drain off all the oil into a container. Measure out 2 tablespoons of the oil and return it to the cast-iron frying pan. Turn the heat to medium-high. Add flour and cook for a few minutes, whisking, until a paste is formed and there are no lumps in the flour.

Add the wine and the chicken stock. Use a whisk to quickly incorporate the liquid into the flour mixture, ensuring there are no lumps. Bring the mixture up to a simmer. The gravy will get very thick at this point. Scrape the bottom of the pan with a wooden spoon to get all the fond incorporated into the gravy. Add the half-and-half a little at a time until the desired consistency is achieved. You want a thick sauce but not a paste. Season the gravy with salt and pepper, adjusting amounts to taste.

Yield: enough gravy for 2 steaks or for dipping 4 CFS sandwiches

SANDWICH:

Chicken-fried steak, prepared in 4 equal
   pieces (see page 116)

4 good-quality hamburger buns or Kaiser
   rolls, toasted if desired

Mayonnaise

Lettuce

Thinly sliced fresh tomato

Pickled jalapeño peppers

Cheddar cheese

Sliced avocado

Creamy pan gravy (see page 119)

ON EACH BUN, place a piece of chicken-fried
steak and garnish as desired. Serve immediately with small bowls of hot creamy pan gravy
for dipping.

Yield: 4 sandwiches

CHEF BULLA'S NOTES: Cut your steak to the approximate size of the bread you would use. The most common bread would be a round, soft bread with a medium-firm crust, like a good-quality hamburger bun or Kaiser roll. Don't use bread that is too crusty and that you have to work hard to bite through, because you'll end up with a mess when you try to bite through a chewy bun and a fairly chewy fried steak with a delicate crust. Similarly, if you use soft white sandwich bread, you wouldn't have enough support for the chicken-fried steak, and the result would be a fairly messy experience. The way I happen to like my CFS sandwich is simple—with mayo, lettuce, and good fresh tomato. I also like having a small side of gravy in a bowl large enough to dip into, like a Texas French Dip. You can treat chicken-fried steak like a burger and top it with whatever you like. Good combinations are pickled jalapeño and cheddar cheese, or avocado with lettuce and tomato.

WHERE TO GO:

Popular Houston locations for CFS sandwiches include Goodson's Café in Tomball (just outside Houston), which is known for serving the biggest "legal" chicken-fried steak in the state.

Goodson's Café
27931 State Highway 249
Tomball, TX 77375
(281) 351-1749

UTAH

During the early 1900s, Italian emigrants continued arriving in America, spreading out across the country in search of employment. Many headed for Utah, beckoned by jobs in the coal and copper mines as well as on the railroad. In 1913, Rosario and Christina Caputo emigrated from the town of Ariello in Calabria, Italy, and set their sights on Salt Lake City, where Rosario found work in the coal mines. By the early 1920s, the Caputos were able to open a small grocery store, a venture that turned out to be fortuitous for later generations of the Caputo family. Their grandson, Tony Caputo, managed a retail food market for many years, and in 1998 he struck out on his own, opening Tony Caputo's Market and Deli. Tony renovated the old Firestone Tire and Rubber Company building adjacent to Salt Lake City's once-dilapidated Pioneer Park, and two years later, he purchased another building. As part of his renovation and development efforts, Tony enticed other businesses into the area, which today includes a farmers' market, a fish company, and a bakery. Pioneer Park Marketplace, as it's now called, has become a major shopping attraction for the culinary inclined.

At Tony Caputo's Market and Deli, shoppers in search of fine ingredients find a utopia for quality products that include imported meats, cheeses, pastas, vinegars, and olive oils. In the past few years, **Salt Lake City Weekly** has voted Tony Caputo's as the source of the best sandwiches in Utah. That award comes as no surprise to patrons who flock to Tony's in search of gourmet sandwiches like the Caputo, created by Tony's son Matthew. Watch carefully and you'll see patrons wrapping their hands lovingly around Tony's sandwiches, often cuddling up to the Caputo as though it were a teddy bear. Well, okay, that's a bit extreme, but you get the idea. This is no ordinary Italian cold-cut sandwich. Top-quality meats and cheese, including imported prosciutto, are dressed with light olive oil and Antica Italia's balsamic vinegar. Accompanied by Sicilian marinated olives and pepperoncini, it's a tribute to the Caputos' Italian heritage and a special treat for diners on the prowl for the best in Utah. Some 400 patrons, purchasing an average of 600 sandwiches a day, can't be wrong.

EAGLE GATE LOOKING TOWARDS STATE CAPITOL

THE CAPUTO

Reprinted with permission from Tony Caputo's Market and Deli,
Salt Lake City, Utah

1 crusty peasant bread roll, 6 to 8 inches in length, sliced through the middle

1 ounce olive oil

1 ounce quality balsamic vinegar, such as Antica Italia

1 1/2 ounces paper-thin slices mortadella (Italian bologna)

1 1/2 ounces thinly sliced Genoa salami

1 ounce paper-thin slices imported prosciutto

1 1/2 ounces thinly sliced provolone cheese

4 thick slices fresh tomato

Several lettuce leaves

Sicilian marinated olives and pepperoncini

PLACE THE BREAD on a cutting board and drizzle one half with the olive oil and the other half with the balsamic vinegar, covering the entire cut surface of the bread. Fold the mortadella in half and distribute evenly on the bottom half of the roll. Add the Genoa salami and the prosciutto, followed by the provolone cheese. Top with the sliced tomato and lettuce leaves, cover with the top half of the bread, and slice the sandwich in half. Garnish with Sicilian marinated olives and pepperoncini and serve.

Yield: 1 sandwich

WHERE TO GO:

If you're in the Salt Lake City area, Tony Caputo's is a must-stop for the finest in Italian foods as well as specialty cooking utensils and handmade pottery.

Tony Caputo's Market and Deli
308 West 300 South Street
Salt Lake City, UT 84101
(801) 531-8669

SCOTT FLETCHER'S CHEESE DREAM SANDWICH

Reprinted with permission from Grafton Village Cheese Company, Grafton, Vermont

4 slices quality white sandwich bread

Slices of Grafton cheddar cheese, sufficient to cover two slices of bread

2 eggs

2 tablespoons milk

4 tablespoons butter

Vermont maple syrup

LAY OUT 2 SLICES of bread and cover each with slices of cheddar cheese; top with remaining bread. Lightly press sandwiches together. Whisk the eggs and milk together until frothy and place the mixture in a shallow dish or pie plate.

In a 12-inch frying pan, melt butter over medium heat. Dip each sandwich in the egg batter, letting the excess drip off, and place it in the frying pan. Fry sandwiches over medium heat until golden brown on each side, turning only once. Slice sandwiches in half or quarters, and serve with Vermont maple syrup for dipping.

Yield: 2 sandwiches

NEED A QUICK FIX?

The Grafton Village Cheese Company will ship its cheese products as well as pure Vermont maple syrup anywhere in the country.

WHERE TO GO:

Grafton Village Cheese Company
P.O. Box 87
533 Townshend Road
Grafton, VT 05146
(802) 843-2221
(800) 472-3866 toll free
www.graftonvillagecheese.com

Rick's Tavern
386 Route 30
Newfane, VT 05345
(802) 365-9784

The tiny town of Grafton in southeastern Vermont is home to the Grafton Village Cheese Company, producers of award-winning cheddar cheese that has become so well known and acclaimed that Grafton's head cheesemaker, Scott Fletcher, was even featured in **Gourmet** magazine's February 1997 issue. "Fletch," as he's known locally, is a true craftsman who has been hand-making Grafton's cheese for more than thirty-six years.

Grafton's cheese heritage dates back to 1890, when the Grafton Cooperative Cheese Company was established to make use of surplus milk from local dairy farms. The company went out of business following a devastating fire that destroyed the factory, but in the mid-1960s, the Windham Foundation, which supports various Vermont preservation activities, restored it as the Grafton Village Cheese Company. Product offerings include natural cheddars that are aged from one to three years, as well as cheddars flavored with smoked maple wood, garlic, or sage. Word of the quality of Grafton's cheese has spread rapidly, and the company ships its products all over the country, including Hawaii, where it's used in the focaccia at Mama's Fish House (see page 35).

Grafton's retail shop offers a full line of the company's cheese. Although they don't serve meals at the Grafton

Village Cheese Company, Scott Fletcher's recipe for Cheese Dream Sandwiches provides a true taste of Vermont, including not only Grafton cheese but the state's famous maple syrup.

Rick's Tavern in nearby Newfane, with its dining booths and firehouse memorabilia, is a fun place to eat, and many

LONG TRAIL LODGE KILLINGTON SECTION, LONG TRAIL, VT. 1

104004

patrons opt for the terrific Vermont Cheddar Steak Sandwich composed of sliced Porterhouse steak, mushrooms, and Grafton cheddar cheese served on a short grinder roll. Rick's Tavern also offers their private label Old Fashioned Root Beer to enjoy in-house or in four-packs to go.

SMOKED TURKEY AND COUNTRY HAM SALAD SANDWICH

Reprinted with permission from Shelley Matrana and Dan and Barbara Gill, Something Different Country Store, Urbanna, Virginia

SALAD:

1 1/2 pounds (3 cups) chopped smoked turkey

1 pound (2 cups) finely chopped or ground cooked country ham

6 hard-boiled eggs, peeled and chopped

1/2 cup finely diced onion

1/2 cup finely chopped celery

1/3 cup prepared yellow mustard

1 cup quality mayonnaise

1/2 cup sweet pickle relish

1 teaspoon granulated or dried minced garlic

1 tablespoon dried parsley

Seasoned salt (use caution) and freshly ground black pepper to taste

IN A LARGE BOWL, mix all salad ingredients together, except salt and pepper, until well combined. Carefully season to taste with the salt and pepper, bearing in mind that country ham is plenty salty on its own. Cover and refrigerate until ready to use.

Yield: About 10 cups, enough for 10 hoagie rolls

NOTE: Commercially available hickory-smoked turkey topped with crushed pepper is excellent in this recipe; reduce or eliminate the ground black pepper. This salad may also be served on its own as a luncheon entrée.

WASHINGTON MONUMENT AND HOTEL RICHMOND, RICHMOND, VA.

Pork and Southern cooking are synonymous, and nowhere in the South is this more true than in Virginia, home of the legendary Smithfield ham. Here, cooks are justifiably proud to serve the local ham, as expressed in this quote from **The Smithfield Cookbook,** published by the Junior Women's Club of Smithfield: "This is, of course, no ordinary ham. It is the Smithfield Ham, praised as quite simply the world's finest. The Smithfield ham is distinguished by its dark red meat, the yellow translucent fat indicative of a peanut-fed hog, a slightly oily texture and its salty but divine flavor. So distinctive are these hams that they are shipped all over the world to grace the finest tables. Queen Victoria, as have other heads of state, ordered the hams on a regular basis."

Indeed. Smithfield ham is American country ham at its finest. It's dry-cured and aged for up to five months, and its taste is defined by a higher salt content than wet-cured hams injected with a salt solution or soaked in brine. Traditionally, Smithfield ham is served very thinly sliced with tiny beaten biscuits, so-called because the dough is beaten with a rolling pin or wooden mallet until it blisters, a process that takes upwards of a half hour, before being cut into one and one-half-inch rounds and baked.

Although Smithfield is Virginia's most well-known location to enjoy the region's famous country ham, a bit of research will lead discriminating palates to hidden dining treasures throughout the state. One such gem is the Something Different Country Store near the historic town of Urbanna, Virginia, located on the Rappahannock River on Virginia's Middle Peninsula. Urbanna was founded in 1680 as a port for tobacco shipments to England. Today, the small town hosts the annual Urbanna Oyster Festival and serves as a destination for year-round visitors in search of great food, including Virginia's ham biscuits.

A foray just a few miles out of Urbanna, in the direction of Remlik, leads to downtown Pinetree, population of about fifteen, and the Something Different Country Store and Deli, one of the few surviving 1940s country stores in the state. Dan and Barbara Gill, local farmers, purchased the property and opened the place for business in 2002 as a showcase for their barbecue, cured and smoked meats, and delicious sandwiches. The Gills are dedicated to the preservation of Virginia traditions and foodways, but the local cuisine is complemented by a healthy dose of specialties from other regions, including a few Louisiana specialties that are whipped up by Shelley Matrana.

Of special interest are items like smoked turkey, slowly smoked North Carolina-style pork barbecue served with a vinegar-based sauce, and smoked salmon served with a Norwegian dill sauce; but other specialties include homemade cottage cheese, breads and spreads, quality cheese, an array of specialty sauces, fresh-roasted coffees, and fine wines.

Dan's Virginia heritage includes a long tradition of curing and smoking real country hams, and he is well versed in the art of producing a quality product. Although Dan doesn't sell his own country ham at the store, there is country ham on the menu, and it's showcased in myriad ways, including a country ham-and-cheese sandwich that has garnered rave reviews. Dan is fond of repeating the old Virginia adage, "Eternity has been defined as two people and a country ham," because frugal folks waste nothing when it comes to such a delicious treat. At Something Different, scraps are ground up and used to make their signature, old-fashioned ham cakes. And if visitors are super-lucky, they'll arrive on a day when there's something "really different" on the menu—such as the perfectly paired smoked turkey and country-cured ham salad sandwich.

SANDWICH:

1/2 to 1 cup salad (see page 126)

Choice of bread or rolls, toasted if desired

Lettuce

SPREAD SALAD on a choice of bread or rolls and top with a few leaves of crispy lettuce. Hoagie rolls require 1 cup of salad; if using standard rolls or bread, consider halving this recipe as only 1/2 cup of salad is required per sandwich.

Yield: 2 traditional sandwiches or 1 hoagie sandwich

NEED A QUICK FIX?

Smithfield hams can be ordered from:

The Smithfield Shoppe
224 Main Street
Smithfield, VA 23430
(757) 357-1790
(800) 628-2242 toll free
www.smithfieldhams.com

WHERE TO GO:

Something Different Country Store
Downtown Pinetree (at Routes 602 and 603)
3617 Old Virginia Street
Urbanna, VA 23175
(804) 758-8000
www.velvitoil.com/roastery.htm

Washington's food heritage is inextricably linked to salmon. For centuries, the livelihood and culture of the Lummi tribe, located at the northern end of Puget Sound, has relied on salmon fishing. At Tillicum Village, located on Blake Island, the ancestral home of the Suquamish Indian tribe, tourists enjoy smoked salmon prepared on cedar stakes placed over alderwood fires, an ancient culinary art practiced by the Native Americans of the Northwest. Visitors and locals alike make the trek to Seattle's historic Pike Place Market, established in 1907, where a host of fishmongers and restaurants feature salmon and other regional specialties.

Hungry market visitors with a penchant for delicious salmon and other Northwest specialties head for Matt's at the Market, a tiny gem of a restaurant tucked away on the third floor of the Corner Market Building. Owner Matt Janke and Chef Erik Cannella produce magical meals based on seasonal produce and the fresh catch-of-the-day from specialty suppliers downstairs. Fantastic views of the Market and Elliott Bay are enhanced by the friendliness of the staff, and not to be missed is Chef Cannella's Salmon BLT, periodically offered as a special on the restaurant's seasonal menu.

SPICY MAYONNAISE:

1 cup prepared mayonnaise

2 tablespoons sambel olek (Vietnamese chili paste) (see note at right)

COMBINE INGREDIENTS and set aside or refrigerate for later use.

SEASONED CORNMEAL CRUST MIXTURE:

$1/4$ cup white cornmeal

2 tablespoons Panko (Japanese breadcrumbs)

$1/4$ teaspoon dried thyme leaves

$1/4$ teaspoon dried oregano

$1/4$ teaspoon salt

$1/2$ teaspoon freshly ground black pepper

$3/4$ teaspoon chile powder

COMBINE INGREDIENTS in a food processor and blend well. Place in a wide bowl or pie plate or turn out onto a large piece of waxed paper.

WHERE TO GO:

Matt's at the Market
94 Pike Street, Suite 32
Seattle, WA 98101
(206) 467-7909

MATT'S AT THE MARKET SALMON BLT

Reprinted with permission from Chef Erik Cannella, Matt's at the Market, Seattle, Washington

SANDWICH:

4 (6-ounce) skinless salmon fillets

Salt and freshly ground black pepper to taste

Seasoned cornmeal crust mixture (see left)

Olive oil

8 slices quality potato bread

Spicy mayonnaise (see far left)

Fresh arugula, washed and dried

12 slices fresh tomato

12 slices bacon, fried crisp and drained

NOTE: If sambel olek is not available, substitute spicy Thai chili sauce, which is commonly available in supermarkets.

SEASON SALMON fillets with salt and pepper to taste. Dredge fillets in the seasoned cornmeal crust mixture and set aside.

In a 12-inch frying pan, add enough olive oil to coat the bottom of the pan. Heat the oil to a low smoke, add salmon fillets, and fry them, turning once. The length of time to cook depends upon the thickness of the fillets and the desired degree of doneness. Be careful not to overcook the salmon.

While salmon is frying, spread each slice of potato bread with the spicy mayonnaise on one side. On each of 4 slices of bread, place arugula leaves to cover and add 3 slices of tomato and 3 slices of bacon to each. Add the fried salmon fillets, cover with remaining slices of bread, slice the sandwiches in half, and serve immediately.

Yield: 4 sandwiches

State Capitol, Charleston, W. Va. — D-19

Fairmont, located in north-central West Virginia, is the pepperoni roll capital of the world. The pepperoni roll is one of those portable, hand-held meals, like Michigan's pasty, created for coal miners who needed a warm, comforting taste of home kitchens while working deep underground. Coal mining in Fairmont dates back to 1835, and by the year 1900, it was the economic backbone of the area. Demand for labor brought emigrants from eastern and southern Europe, including many Italians.

According to local legend, Giuseppe Argiro, the original proprietor of the Country Club Bakery, created the pepperoni roll in 1927. A former miner, Argiro was inspired to produce the rolls after noticing that many of his co-workers carried pepperoni and bread in their lunch pails. Argiro decided to enclose sticks of pepperoni in his rolls and then bake them, producing hot, slightly moist and sweet rolls redolent with the sausage's spiciness. Pepperoni rolls subsequently became a popular portable meal throughout the state. They are still made today and sold at the Country Club Bakery as well as in supermarkets, gas stations, convenience stores, and even newsstands.

At Colasessano's, a popular take-out shop in Fairmont, the pepperoni roll has been elevated to a gustatory delight. The foot-long roll is about double the size of its competitors, and variations contain not just pepperoni but provolone cheese and roasted peppers as well. Colasessano's pepperoni rolls are typically served open-face, topped with a delectable tomato-based meat sauce.

Tim Dotson, a former West Virginian now living in Florida, quickly discovered that pepperoni rolls aren't ubiquitous to the rest of the country. In order to satisfy his craving, Tim developed a recipe that has earned him fame, if not fortune, among new friends and colleagues, and he generously agreed to share it.

DOUGH:

$1/4$ cup sugar

1 package dry yeast

1 teaspoon salt

$1/4$ cup dry powdered milk

$1 1/2$ cups warm water

4 cups flour

IN A LARGE BOWL, mix the sugar, yeast, salt, and powdered milk, and then add the warm water, stirring to dissolve the dry ingredients. Stir in the flour, using extra flour or water as needed to make a soft dough that isn't too sticky. Turn out onto a floured board and knead for a couple of minutes. Shape dough into a ball, place in a lightly greased bowl, cover with a towel, and let the dough rise for 30 minutes to 1 hour, or until doubled in bulk.

TIM'S PEPPERONI ROLLS

Reprinted with permission from Tim Dotson, West Virginia native and pepperoni roll fan, now living in DeBary, Florida

SANDWICH:

60 paper-thin slices (about 4 ounces) of packaged pepperoni

3 cups grated mozzarella cheese (optional)

1 egg

1 tablespoon water

TIM'S NOTES: I always double the recipe (just use twice as much of everything, except one package of yeast is fine). A dozen rolls will make four people very happy. If you want to be creative, add cheese or roasted red pepper before baking, or omit the pepperoni and use something else. And, to make a good quantity for trips or to freeze, quadruple everything (except just use 2 packages of yeast); you'll need a 5-pound bag of flour.

Yield: 4 to 6 dozen rolls that freeze well and heat up quickly in the microwave

WHERE TO GO:

Country Club Bakery
1211 Country Club Road
Fairmont, WV 26554
(304) 363-5690

Colasessano's
506 Pennsylvania Avenue
Fairmont, WV 26554
(304) 363-9713

PREHEAT THE OVEN to 425 degrees. Turn the dough out onto a lightly floured board, punch it down, and cut it into 12 equal pieces. With your hand, lightly flatten each piece on the board into an oblong shape, about 8 inches in length, and place 5 slices of pepperoni down the middle, overlapping but not stacked. If using the cheese, sprinkle about 2 tablespoons on top of the pepperoni. Fold the short sides inward, then roll it up like a jelly roll, ensuring that no pepperoni or cheese is sticking out. Place the rolls at least 1 inch apart on ungreased baking sheets.

In a small bowl, beat together the egg and water and lightly brush the mixture over the rolls. You don't need to let the rolls rise farther, but you can if you want to. Bake the rolls until golden brown, about 20 to 25 minutes. Cool for 5 minutes and serve.

Yield: 12 (6-inch long) pepperoni rolls

Sheboygan, Wisconsin, the "Wurst City in the World," is formally known as the "Bratwurst Capital of the World." Indeed, the city's bratwurst, a spicy, fresh pork sausage, is so popular throughout the state that the Wisconsin legislature declared a "Sheboygan double bratwurst on a hard roll, with the works . . . the ultimate state sandwich." And nowhere is the brat taken more seriously than in Sheboygan where an annual festival, Bratwurst Days, is held in its honor every August.

The bratwurst in America dates back to the early 1800s. Thousands of German emigrants made their way to Wisconsin and America's heartland, attracted by the lush agricultural lands, in the latter part of the nineteenth century. The region became known for its grain and hog production, facilitating the eventual establishment of the butcher shops and meat-packing plants that are a hallmark of the region. Those Germans who settled in Wisconsin introduced bratwurst and a host of other traditional sausages. Although Sheboygan is noted for the sausage, with several meat markets specializing in bratwurst, it's also made in numerous other locations throughout the state.

The original bratwurst is a delicately spiced, fresh pork sausage, but in recent years, manufacturers have introduced new varieties like onion, garlic, and jalapeño-cheddar bratwurst. Most bratwurst comes in a tubular casing, but sausage patties are also available. Wisconsinites recommend buying the fresh, or at least frozen-fresh, bratwurst versus the precooked type.

With two locations offering a great charcoal-grilled bratwurst, the Charcoal Inn has established a formidable presence in Sheboygan. The sandwiches are typically served oozing with melted butter, a quirky, delicious preference among folks in the area. Most patrons order the official Wisconsin state version that calls for two bratwursts on a single hard roll with mustard, onion, and pickles.

Some cooks advocate boiling the sausage in beer before grilling, while others flatly state the need to carefully grill it until the sausage is crusty on the outside and still juicy on the inside. A few taverns simply steam or poach their brats. No matter how they are cooked, bratwurst fans are adamant about using crusty hard rolls, also of German origin, for construction of a brat sandwich. Sauerkraut is another popular option.

NEED A QUICK FIX?

If you can't make a brat-run to Sheboygan, Meisfeld's will ship their grand champion bratwurst.

Miesfeld's Meat Market
4811 Venture Avenue
Sheboygan, WI 53081
(920) 565-6328
www.miesfelds.com

GRILLED BRATS, SHEBOYGAN-STYLE

BRATWURST:

4 fresh bratwurst sausages

1 (12-ounce) can or bottle of beer (do not use light beer)

PIERCE EACH BRATWURST four times with a fork and place in a pan large enough to hold them in one layer. Add beer, bring to a boil over medium heat, and let simmer for 15 to 20 minutes.

Heat grill. Drain bratwurst and place on grill over medium-high heat. Grill bratwurst for about 10 minutes, or until well browned.

WHERE TO GO:

The Charcoal Inn has two locations:

1637 Geele Avenue
Sheboygan, WI 53083
(920) 458-1147

1313 South Eighth Street
Sheboygan, WI 53081
(920) 458-6988

SANDWICH:

Softened butter

4 bratwurst rolls, crusty rolls, or hot dog rolls

4 grilled bratwurst (see left)

German or Dijon-style mustard (or mustard of choice)

Chopped fresh onion

Pickles

Sauerkraut (optional)

LIGHTLY BUTTER THE ROLLS. Just before brats are done, place rolls under a preheated broiler, or facedown on the grill, until they are golden brown. Place brats in rolls and serve with mustard, onion, and pickles or sauerkraut, if desired.

Yield: 4 sandwiches

NOTE: Sheboyganites are likely to douse their bratwurst sandwiches with plenty of hot melted butter.

In 1993, Dick Hoover decided that he needed to escape the heat of Dallas summers, so he bought a dilapidated old building in Story, fixing it up into what his wife, Patty, says looks a bit like the Alamo. Two years after opening the store, Patty rolled out her moose-themed restaurant, cleverly named the Waldorf A'Story. Both the store and the restaurant are open every day of the year except Christmas.

During the summer, patrons can dine outdoors amidst splendid views of the Big Horn Mountains. Among a host of delicious sandwiches and sophisticated specials, the Moosey Breakfast Samich has attracted a loyal following.

The Piney Creek General Store in Story, Wyoming, is filled chock-a-block with an enormous range of miscellaneous paraphernalia that includes groceries, gourmet cooking ingredients, beer and wine, cast-iron cookware, and kitschy souvenirs and gifts. The store also has a tiny restaurant called the Waldorf A'Story, and savvy travelers on Interstate 90 between Sheridan and Buffalo, Wyoming, know that it's smart business to schedule a stop here for a bite to eat. As the menu reminds diners, it's only eight to ten minutes from the highway, "Longer from New York . . . but take yer time . . . yer in God's country!"

MOOSEY BREAKFAST SAMICH

Reprinted with permission from Patty Hoover, owner, Waldorf A'Story, Story, Wyoming

2 slices quality sourdough bread

Butter

2 eggs

2 slices American cheese

4 slices cooked bacon, 1 slice fried ham, or 2 fried pork sausage patties

Thinly sliced raw purple onion to taste

2 slices fresh tomato

BUTTER ONE SIDE of each slice of bread and brown the bread, buttered side down, in a frying pan or on a grill over low heat. While the bread browns, fry the eggs, scrambling them slightly. Place cheese on top of the eggs and cover just long enough to melt the cheese. Place one piece of the bread on a serving plate, add the cooked meat of choice and top with eggs and cheese, and onion, and tomato. Cover the sandwich with the remaining slice of bread, cut the sandwich in half, stick a toothpick in each half to hold them together, and serve immediately.

Yield: 1 sandwich

WHERE TO GO:

Piney Creek General Store/Waldorf A'Story
19 North Piney Road
Story, WY 82842
(307) 683-2400

Sandwich Index

126–29; and Country Ham Salad Sandwich, Smoked, 126–29

Villa Basque Deli's Chorizo Sausage Sandwich, 79

Walleye Sandwich, Minnesota Fried, 68–69
Water chestnuts, 73
Wheat pocket pita breads, 19

State Index

SANDWICHES THAT YOU WILL LIKE

The saucy PBS program toasting the crusty glory of American sandwiches on DVD and VHS

See the tasty TV special!

Producer Rick Sebak (who also brought you "A Hot Dog Program" and "An Ice Cream Show") and his crusty crew travel from Maine to California looking for incredible American sandwiches. Have a pastrami in New York City. Sample a Maid Rite "loosemeat" in Iowa, a St. Paul sandwich in St. Louis and a chipped ham "Slammer" in Pittsburgh. How about barbecued brisket in Texas? Or Italian beef in Chicago? Try a muffuletta and several shrimp and oyster po-boys in New Orleans. And see why folks in Buffalo go for a beef-on-weck while people in Louisville love a Hot Brown!

DVD (with over 40 minutes of bonus material) and VHS
$19.95 each plus shipping & handling and applicable sales tax

To order your copy of **Sandwiches That You Will Like**
Call 1-800-274-1307 or visit Shop WQED at www.wqed.org

WQED
Multimedia
PITTSBURGH